Leading the
Virtual Workforce

Leading the Virtual Workforce

How Great Leaders Transform Organizations in the 21st Century

Karen Sobel **Lojeski**
with Richard R. **Reilly**

WILEY

John Wiley & Sons, Inc.

Published by John Wiley & Sons, Inc., Hoboken, New Jersey.
Published simultaneously in Canada.

For general information on our other products and services or for technical support, please contact our Customer Care Department within the United States at (800) 762-2974, outside the United States at (317) 572-3993 or fax (317) 572-4002.

Wiley also publishes its books in a variety of electronic formats. Some content that appears in print may not be available in electronic books. For more information about Wiley products, visit our web site at www.wiley.com.

Library of Congress Cataloging-in-Publication Data

Sobel Lojeski, Karen.
   Leading the virtual workforce : how great leaders transform organizations in the 21st century / Karen Sobel Lojeski, Richard R. Reilly.
       p. cm. – (Microsoft executive leadership series ; 14)
   Includes index.
Summary: "How to understand and attain the attributes and skills required to be a successful leader in the new digital age. Rapidly evolving changes in the way that we work have led to the need for a new model of leadership. Motivating and inspiring employees who are geographically, culturally, and functionally dispersed requires new sets of skills and different kinds of behaviors. This visionary book uses real-life models of world-class leaders who have demonstrated their ability to lead their virtual workforce through the combined use of technology and personal styles. It presents a new model of leadership that incorporates the key attributes of these successful leaders and presents tools and techniques for becoming a successful leader in the digital age. Karen Sobel Lojeski, PhD (Port Jefferson, NY), is Professor in the Department of Technology and Society in the College of Engineering and Applied Sciences at the State University of New York at Stony Brook. Karen is also the CEO of Virtual Distance International, an advisory firm specializing in leadership and innovation in the new millenium virtual workplace. Richard R. Reilly, PhD (Basking Ridge, NJ), is Emeritus Professor of Technology Management at Stevens Institute of Technology"–Provided by publisher.
   ISBN 978-0-470-42280-9
   1. Leadership.   2. Computers–Social aspects.   I. Reilly, Richard R.   II. Title.
   HD57.7.S6925 2010
   658.4′092–dc22

                                                                2009025055

Printed in the United States of America

10 9 8 7 6 5 4 3 2 1

For Edward Friedman and A.J. Lederman

Contents

Microsoft Executive Leadership Series: Series Foreword

Today's world requires lifelong learning. The Microsoft Executive Leadership Series provides leaders with access to new ideas and perspectives, intended to inspire and to challenge—ideas that will help keep thoughts fresh and minds nimble. These ideas range from effective strategy to deploying an agile infrastructure. Information technology increasingly drives the evolution of business models, social norms, market expansion, even the very shape and nature of our institutions. Organizations that succeed in the future will differentiate themselves effectively on how well they use technology to navigate change, respond to challenges, and leverage new opportunities.

I talk nearly every day to executives and policy makers grappling with issues like globalization, workforce evolution, and the impact of technology on people and processes. The idea for this series came from those conversations—we see the series as a way to distill what we've learned as a company into actionable intelligence. The authors bring independent perspectives, expertise, and experience. We hope their insights will spark dialogues within organizations, among managers, and with policy makers about the critical relationship between people and technology in the workplace of tomorrow.

I hope you enjoy this title in the Microsoft Executive Leadership Series and find it useful as you plan for the expected and unexpected developments ahead. It's our privilege and our commitment to be part of that conversation.

DANIEL W. RASMUS

General Editor, Microsoft Executive Leadership Series

Titles in the Executive Leadership Series:

Rules to Break and Laws to Follow by Don Peppers and Martha Rogers, 2008.

Generation Blend by Rob Salkowitz, 2008.

Uniting the Virtual Workforce by Karen Sobel Lojeski and Richard R. Reilly, 2008.

Drive Business Performance by Bruno Aziza and Joey Fitts, 2008.

Listening to the Future by Daniel W. Rasmus with Rob Salkowitz, 2008.

Business Prosperity by Michael Hugos, 2009.

Strategic Project Portfolio Management by Simon Moore, 2009

Leading the Virtual Workforce by Karen Sobel Lojeski and with Richard R. Reilly, 2009.

Old World, Young World by Rob Salkowitz, 2010.

Preface

A few years ago, Warren Bennis, a prominent leadership scholar noted the following:

> Bad leadership at Enron alone impoverished thousands of employees, stealing their livelihoods, gutting their retirement accounts, and tearing them apart with stress.... There are, no doubt, people who took their own lives because of what was done at Enron by its lavishly compensated bad leaders.[1]

As it turns out Bennis underestimated the impact that bad leadership can have. A combination of greed, hubris, flawed judgment, and miscalculation has made the Enron debacle seem almost quaint by comparison to the global financial crisis that we now face. Although numerous pundits and scholars have advanced many reasons for the devastating situation, the bottom line is, as Bennis pointed out previously, bad leadership is one of the major reasons for the current state of affairs. However, it's not simply dreadful leadership, it's also *the wrong kind* of leadership for a new age.

If a group of typical corporate employees from the early 1980s could be time-transported into today's interconnected, high tech, global world they would be astonished by the degree of change in the way that work is done. This same group of employees might also be surprised to learn that the same leadership models they learned about in the early 1980s are pretty much still applied in our academic institutions and our business enterprises, without any significant modifications or alterations to address the challenges leaders face in the digital age.

---

[1] W. Bennis, "The Challenges of Leadership in the Modern World," *American Psychologist*, 62, 2–5.

In the first book, *Uniting the Virtual Workforce*,[2] a new phenomenon was described. It's called Virtual Distance. And it explains much of what had been highly misunderstood about the virtual workforce until then. The Virtual Distance model also shines much needed light onto what leaders of today need to do differently.

Virtual Distance is characterized by a combination of physical separation, technology mediation, and disconnected relationships. These dynamics lead to a psychological separation that builds over time. And the research documents the negative effects that Virtual Distance can have on productivity, innovation, and trust between employees and groups of organizations. This data should be of major interest to any leader trying to improve performance and advance competitive advantage.

When Virtual Distance is relatively high the following critical success factors significantly degrade:

- Innovation falls by over 90% and competitive advantage is severely impacted.
- On-time/on-budget project performance suffers by over 50% and can cost a company millions of dollars.
- Trust declines by over 80%.
- Job satisfaction drops off by over 80%.
- Goal and role clarity decline by over 60%.
- Good citizenship behavior plummets by over 70%.

These results, which reflect outcomes in over 500 project teams from around the world, quantitatively show that the virtual workforce needs new leader focus. The original Virtual Distance research approach included interviews with dozens of managers, individuals, and leaders. Than, a survey was deployed to measure the Virtual Distance Index among hundreds of teams. Using this data, it was found that:

- Virtual Distance has significant impact on performance and competitive outcomes.

---

[2]K. Sobel Lojeski, R. Reilly, *Uniting the Virtual Workforce: Transforming Leadership and Innovation in the Globally Integrated Enterprise* (Hoboken, NJ: John Wiley & Sons, 2008).

- Virtual Distance is not only measurable but can also be predicted, therefore it can be avoided with proper analysis, planning, or intervention.
- Virtual Distance is just as prevalent among co-located team members as it is among geographically dispersed groups so it should not be assumed that if you have people all working in the same place you are without Virtual Distance risk.
- When Virtual Distance is relatively high—leader performance suffers significantly more than when Virtual Distance is relatively low.

These findings have been used to help organizations improve performance, enhance innovation, and avoid problems before they emerge through Virtual Distance Indexing, Virtual Distance Mapping, and Virtual Distance Management, techniques detailed in the first book on the subject.

Survey research, which led to the ability to quantitatively measure the impact of Virtual Distance, is a powerful method for uncovering important information. But surveys are also limited in that they don't give the whole story or allow for immediate follow-up when something interesting is found.

So in this follow-on work another approach was used. Interviews were taken with highly effective executives as well as other thought-leaders. The major participants, in order of their first appearance in the book, include:

- Steven A. Tainer, Contemplation Scholar and Author
- Susan Roser, Senior Vice President, Global Service Support, Western Union
- Robert McMahon, President of U.S. Commercial Operations, Merck & Co., Inc.
- Cheri Sterman, Director of Child Development and Consumer Relationships, Crayola
- Guido Petit, Director of Alcatel-Lucent Technical Academy, Alcatel-Lucent

- Gina Poole, Vice President of IBM Software Group Marketing 2.0, IBM
- Philip McKinney, Vice President and CTO, Personal Systems Group, Hewlett Packard Company
- Kathy Burke-Thomas, Associate Director, AT&T Project Management Center of Excellence, AT&T
- Lawrence A. McAndrews, CEO, NACHRI (National Association of Children's Hospitals and Related Institutions)
- Jack Barsky, Vice President of Information Technology, NRG
- Piet Hut, Professor, Institute for Advanced Study in Princeton, New Jersey

One of the greatest challenges, as well as greatest opportunities in writing this book, was the wealth of material and insight collected. Ultimately the analysis of this information led to the development of the *Virtual Distance Leadership Model*—comprised of the most salient features of the strategies and tactics used by the best to lead the virtual workforce. At the core of the model are three core competencies:

1. Creating Context
2. Cultivating Community
3. Co-Activating New Leaders

The ability to create a common context for employees, contractors, part-timers, interns, and others in the virtual workforce was a key characteristic of the leaders interviewed and others studied. What is meant by context? It is everything around us that helps us to understand who we are, where we are and what our role is. Context is the foundation upon which we derive meaning from what other people say.

In the past, the requisite context needed to do a good job was readily available. We commuted from home to work, coworkers knew where we lived, how many children we had, what our marital status was, approximately how old we were, and so on. We went to an office every day and saw the same people. We knew a lot about our boss, and the boss's boss and that helped us see how we fit into the organization and what our career path might look like. We saw people day after day and knew about not only their work lives but their personal lives as well. With that information we could cipher who thought what about work as well as politics, family, and other important notions in life. And from there we could determine our relative positions and adjust our behaviors and strategies to best serve ourselves as well as the organization.

But today it's not so simple. We may never see our boss and co-workers face-to-face. A lot of our work is done in temporary projects where people come and go, and organizational affiliations change with each new project or merger or downsizing. Our physical space can be a remote office, or even a space in our home. Others' view of life beyond work is often shielded by electronic gizmos and we may never know how someone feels about some of the very things that we care about most.

And while it might be easy, neat and logical to think that we don't need such things to stay on task, that's just not the case. That kind of magical thinking has led us astray. It's unrealistic to believe the "hype" that suddenly, given technological tools, we will simply behave in a way that is fully rational, finely tuned, and in synch with others. No. That's just not true. Instead, under such circumstances, people remain highly emotional beings as well as rational workers. When we are blind to others' contexts—their surroundings, the way they think, and more, we simply do not operate with maximum effectiveness. So one of the things that leaders need to do most is to help individuals and teams in the virtual workforce see the context that is otherwise invisible. They do this by understanding how to use technology to communicate effectively and by serving as a human anchor, or constant, to help everyone stay connected.

The second key characteristic, cultivating community, is not one normally associated with corporate leadership. But today much of the work is done by loosely connected individuals who come together in teams to accomplish some objective and then go on to work in other teams or assignments. As organizations have become flatter and more matrixed the ability to "recruit" people to work on projects or other assignments has become an important aspect of leadership. One way that effective leaders do this is by building diverse communities of people who have the skill and commitment to help, even though this may fall outside their prescribed organizational roles. In other words, a lot of what happens to get work done in organizations today is voluntary. Organizational psychologists refer to such voluntary activities as organizational citizenship behaviors because they help maintain the growth and sustainability of the organization in ways that are not role specific. Mentoring others, taking on a project to build a wiki, and acting as a coach are examples. Leaders can create a sense of community that activates a kind of virtual team spirit and produces extraordinary behaviors—even among the most dispersed set of workers.

The final characteristic is called co-activating leadership. A lot of thought was given to the notion of "shared leadership" first. Shared leadership makes sense when you are talking about a project team. Each member can play a leadership role at different times during the project lifecycle, for example. But senior leaders told a different story about working with others. They often lead in an indirect way, using what we call "leader intent" to influence and motivate others to lead. This may come from encouraging employees in a community or it may come from writing an engaging article on a blog that inspires others in a new way. A lot of what these leaders do is outside the usual lines of authority. Instead it relies on influence that comes from their expertise, personal qualities, and a keen understanding that informal networks, as opposed to more traditional formal networks, are the main routes into developing leaders of the future.

Of course there are additional characteristics that enable the three core competencies of the Virtual Distance Leadership Model. One critical aspect is called *techno-dexterity*. This includes not only mastering a keen understanding and facility with different technologies but also knowing what kind of communication technology to use and when to use it. E-mail, teleconferencing, video conferencing, web conferencing, and face-to-face are all available, but the leaders showcased use these applications in a way that matches the need and the significance of the communication. They make a conscious, selective decision depending on the message and it's importance to the receiver.

Another aspect has to do with understanding how to use social networks that can be based on technology-enablement or old-fashioned professional societies. Having a strong, extensive social network allows leaders to build their own communities as well as communities for others, span cultural and geographic boundaries, and identify the right people when an important issue needs to be addressed. And while this aspect of leadership, seen in isolation, is nothing new, with so many choices for how to spend one's time developing these crucial synergies, its not necessarily intuitively obvious, to even the most senior management, what works best. And as is pointed out later, only ten percent of executives use social media on a regular basis—but great leaders experiment and find an optimal mix of in-person and on-line interactions.

One final characteristic for mention here (there are others discussed throughout this book) is authenticity. Today's workforce is very different than the workforce of 20 or even 10 years ago. Authentic leaders are not only genuine, but also transparent. This allows them to create a level of trust and commitment that is essential in leading a multicultural, multi-generational global workforce.

Throughout the book Virtual Distance is discussed. Virtual Distance, if well understood, can provide an ideal road map for leaders on how to increase productivity and innovation. In the Virtual Distance research, it was found unequivocally, that leadership means more in the virtual workforce than it does in a traditional one—it has an even greater impact—both on the positive as well as the negative side. Together with the unprecedented data set collected and the information gathered in the interviews that follow, the *Virtual Distance Leadership Model* is offered.

Virtual Distance Leadership is a breakthrough approach to enhancing innovation and productivity in the virtual workforce. The Virtual Distance Leader transforms organizations, in many ways differently than leaders who have come before them. They are much more successful at increasing financial performance and setting the stage for competitive advantage in the new world of work.

ORGANIZATION OF THE BOOK

In Chapter 1 a brief overview of the myriad of changes that require us to look at leadership differently is discussed. With leadership books available by the hundreds, it was important in this work to focus on "What's Changed," "What's New," and not simply on yet another way to say the same old thing about leadership. Traditional leadership models continue to proliferate but they tend to ignore the fact that the assumptions on which they are built have all but collapsed, creating a whole new set of circumstances that rarely gets mentioned when leadership for today's workforce is discussed. This chapter highlights some of these gaps.

In Chapter 2 a brief history of leadership models is given. Most of the leader models we are familiar with focus on traits, situations, or behaviors. And while some or all of these models may still have some useful life in the new world of virtual work, many of them do not speak to the most fundamental change of all—that we rarely see each other and therefore have little opportunity to use charisma, transformational styles, or any other trait or behavior ideal for the "in-person" world, but not necessarily the virtual world.

Chapter 3 shows how great leaders build context. Three executive interviews are showcased in this chapter; Susan Roser, Senior Vice President of Operations for Western Union, Robert McMahon, President of U.S. Commercial Operations for Merck, Inc. & Co., and Cheri Sterman, Director of Child Development and Consumer Relationships, Crayola.

Chapter 4 details how great leaders cultivate community. Two executive interviews are showcased in this chapter; Guido Petit, Director of Alcatel-Lucent Technical Academy, Alcatel Lucent, and Gina Poole, Vice President of IBM Software Group Marketing 2.0, IBM.

In Chapter 5 co-activating new leaders is discussed. Three more executive interviews are included in this chapter; Philip McKinney, Vice President and CTO—Personal Systems Group, Hewlett Packard Company, Kathy Burke-Thomas, Associate Director, AT&T Project Management Center of Excellence, and Lawrence McAndrews, CEO of

National Association of Children's Hospitals and Related Institutions (NACHRI).

In Chapter 6 the concept of *techno-dexterity* is revealed through discussion and more interviews. Highlighted here is the need for a firm grasp and understanding of technology for leader communications. Many of the executives listed above are quoted about this topic. In addition, Jack Barsky, Vice President of Information Technology at NRG talks about his use of video conferencing and Piet Hut, Director of Interdisciplinary Studies from the Institute for Advanced Study at Princeton is highlighted as a pioneer in using virtual world technology in the scientific and contemplation realms.

In Chapter 7 all of the ideas highlighted come together into a new leadership model for the twenty-first century, The Virtual Distance Leadership Model. Remarks are extended on how the Virtual Distance Leadership Model reduces Virtual Distance fueling higher levels of trust and an increased willingness on the part of individuals and teams to do more for those they follow.

In Chapter 8 the future of leadership in a digital age is discussed. Now more than ever good leaders need to step up, challenge old assumptions, and help forward an agenda that serves the people in the workforce—not just a goal to get as "techno-connected" as possible which actually bears little on how human beings perform at their best.

In Chapter 9 the full interview with Steven Tainer is put forth. Steven is a world-renowned contemplation scholar whose view of leadership is much different than others interviewed. Yet his comments have a great deal of relevance to today's leader and also speak directly to those of us who seek to be better human beings and live a more complete life.

In Appendix A an overview of the Virtual Distance Model is provided. The central tenets of the Virtual Distance Model are highlighted which will help the reader understand more fully how he/she can develop into a great leader in today's world and prepare others for what is yet to come.

About the Interviewees

As mentioned in the Preface, a number of people thought to represent great leaders in the digital age or others who had interesting insights into leadership in a technological world were interviewed extensively. At times their comments are featured in case studies. At other times quotes were used to underline certain key points.

Following are the interviewee profiles. They are listed in order of their first appearance in the book.

Steven A. Tainer

Steven A. Tainer is one of the first students of Tibetan Buddhism in the West. He has studied Eastern contemplative traditions intensively for forty years with many Tibetan, Chinese, and Korean masters. After practicing for a number of years in mountain retreats, he now teaches Buddhist, Taoist, and Confucian views and methods. His specialties are Indian Buddhist philosophy, the "Unity of the Three Traditions" in Chinese thought, Taoist yogic practice, and Ch'an contemplation. One of his main areas of investigation and teaching has been the application and implementation of these traditional insights in modern workaday lay life.

Steven has served on the faculty of the Institute for World Religions and the Berkeley Buddhist Monastery since 1995. He is a faculty member of the Kira Institute (www.kira.org), which explores the interface between modern, scientifically-framed perspectives and matters involving human values. He is also the co-founder and Editor of WoK (www.waysofknowing.net/).

Working on behalf of his teachers, Steven has been the coauthor or editor of over eighteen books on Buddhism and Taoism (including

Dragon's Play, and *Time, Space, Knowledge*). A new series of books on his own teaching is also in progress.

Susan Roser

Senior Vice President, Global Service Support, Western Union

Susan Roser is Senior Vice President, America's Operations for Western Union Financial Services Inc. Ms. Roser has responsibility for overseeing agent operations for North and South America and Anti Money Laundering (AML) compliance operations.

Ms. Roser has 15 years of experience with Western Union / First Data.

Previously, as SVP of Global Service Support, she was responsible for customer service for agents and consumers, management of our global call centers, in addition to AML and Fraud Operations.

She led Operations for TeleCheck, a subsidiary of First Data, where she was responsible for customer service operations and relationship management.

Ms. Roser also worked in the Integrated Payment Systems business where she was the Vice President of Official Check and Money Order Products. In this capacity, she was responsible for sales, service and product development for Official Check and Money Order products for financial institutions.

Prior to First Data, Ms. Roser spent over 13 years in the banking industry where she held various positions in the customer service and operations functions.

Robert McMahon

President of U.S. Commercial Operations, Merck & Co., Inc.

Robert A. McMahon is President of U. S. Commercial Operations at Merck & Co., Inc., where he has worked his way up through a progression of increasing responsibility over the last 25 years. Throughout his career, Bob has developed a reputation as a passionate leader with a keen ability to motivate a diverse employee population scattered throughout the nation. He is also known as a steadfast advocate of Merck's mission of putting patients first.

Mr. McMahon is a graduate of Villanova University where he earned a Bachelor of Science degree in accounting. He began his career with Arthur Andersen & Co. in their New York Office. He also worked at the Squibb Corporation prior to joining Merck.

A CPA by training, Mr. McMahon began his Merck career in finance. Over the course of his career, he has held a variety of commercial roles with both domestic and international responsibilities. From 2000 to 2004, Bob served as Vice President and General Manager of Merck/Schering-Plough Pharmaceuticals. He was then appointed Vice President, Marketing and Franchise Business Group Leader of the Arthritis and Analgesia Franchise Business Group. In 2005, Bob was appointed General Manager, U. S. Human Health, Hospital and Specialty Products and then became General Manager of the Cardiovascular/Metabolic Business Unit. In October 2007, Mr. McMahon was promoted to President, U. S. Pharmaceuticals and in August 2008, Bob assumed his current position as President, U. S. Commercial Operations.

Mr. McMahon and his wife Andrea currently reside in Bucks County, Pennsylvania. They have two adult children.

Cheri Sterman

Director of Child Development and Consumer Relationships, Crayola

Speaking on the behalf of children—helping parents and educators understand children's abilities and interests—has been Cheri Sterman's career.

Cheri Sterman is an experienced child advocate and "kid expert" who helps others understand what children, their parents, and teachers want and need. Cheri taught child development to future teachers at the University of Cincinnati and Sinclair College in Ohio. She lead parenting programs for Head Start and Preschool Enrichment Programs. She's authored Crayola publications entitled, *How Children Learn* and *The Power of Creativity*, helping adults understand children's potential. She's advised policy makers and business leaders on kid trends and child development issues.

She has provided leadership to regional and national child advocacy associations and serves as a spokesperson on children's issues to media, businesses, government, and academic organizations:

- Member of United States White House Committee for Children and Youth, 1984
- Governor Richard Celeste's Director of Children's Programs— setting policies and administering funds to educate and protect children in Ohio, 1984–1987
- Member, Governor's Commission for Children and Families, Ohio 1983–1987, Pennsylvania 1987–1994
- Treasurer for the National Association for the Education of Young Children, 1985–1989
- Governing Board of National Association for Child Development Credentialing, 1985–1989
- Conference Chair for Ohio Children's Defense Fund, 1984–1987
- Child Development Regional Training Director, U.S. Administration of Children, Youth, and Families Child Development, 1980–1984
- Presenter on "State of Childhood Today" for the National Governor's Association, 1986
- United Way's Women's Leadership Initiative, Early Childhood Mentors Program, 2006–2008
- US and Canada satellite media PR tours on Children's Creativity; How Children Learn, and Childhood Today, 2006–2008

Twenty years ago Cheri joined Crayola as the Director of Child Development. She provides "kid expertise" so Crayola products and programs meet children's, parents', and teachers' needs. She guides the company on how to communicate with children and the adults who inspire kids. Cheri supervises the Crayola Editorial-Content Group, assuring a consistent brand voice that's relevant to today's families. She directs the Brand-Consumer Relationship, supervising the Consumer Contact Center, a team that interacts with 350,000 consumers each year.

James McNeal states in his publication, *The Kids Market,* that Cheri Sterman is one of the top five experts in kids marketing. McNeal credits Cheri with having "insightful interpretations of children's thinking and behavior that gives her a sixth sense—a unique way of knowing what children want and need." You can read Cheri's parenting tips on *How to Raise a Creative Child* and *Find Out Your Other IQ*^{TM}—*Imagination Quotient* on Crayola.com.

Credentials—She credits her three kids with teaching her most of what she knows about parenting and child development—yet her academic background is rooted in researching childhood.

Master of Education, Early Childhood, University of Cincinnati, 1977

Bachelor of Science, Child Development and Family Life, University Cincinnati 1976

Bachelor of Science, Education—Elementary and Early Childhood, University of Cincinnati, 1976

Guido Petit

Director of Alcatel-Lucent Technical Academy, Alcatel Lucent

Guido currently leads the Alcatel-Lucent Technical Academy, a program to recognize individuals who have made exceptional contributions to Alcatel-Lucent technological leadership and who volunteer to act as a think tank to come up with proposals to improve R&D effectiveness in domains such as innovation, knowledge sharing and networking. Guido is also secretary (and active member) of the Innovation Board at Alcatel-Lucent in Belgium and is member of the project team responsible for the organization of Entrepreneurial Boot Camps.

Previously, Guido has held various positions in Alcatel (before the merger with Lucent) such as Director of the Network Strategy Group in Antwerp (Belgium) and Plano (Texas, USA), Project Manager of the Network Performance Modeling Group in the Corporate Research Center in Antwerp and Project Lead for Traffic Engineering of Digital Switching Systems.

Guido has published more than 70 papers in leading technical journals/conferences. From 2001 till 2004, he was a visiting professor at the Department of Telecommunications and Information Processing of the University of Ghent (Belgium).

Guido is member of the Scientific Advisory Board of the Expertise Centrum for Digital Media (University of Hasselt–Belgium) and of the Strategic Advisory Board of the Industrial College School in Antwerp.

He holds more than 14 European Patents and he is passionate about improving innovation effectiveness.

Gina Poole

Vice President, IBM Software Group Marketing 2.0, IBM

Gina Poole is Vice President of IBM Software Group Marketing 2.0. She has worldwide responsibility for driving high impact demand generation programs and tactics; transforming the marketing mix to increase use of digital and social media; and leveraging marketing automation and analytics to optimize results. She leads software Web Marketing and Sales; directing a worldwide team to deliver IBM's software web presence, web marketing tactics including social media marketing, and web-based sales channels. Gina also leads the portfolio of software events including thousands of in-person and virtual events ranging from localized sessions to large worldwide conferences. In addition, Gina is responsible for creating and optimizing programs that use IBM social software offerings and technologies to drive innovation, collaboration and productivity. She is charged with establishing IBM as *the showcase* for the benefits of social computing.

In her previous role, she was Vice President, Innovation and University Relations for IBM. She had worldwide responsibility for developing and executing IBM's internal and external innovation programs for collaborating with employees, clients, partners, governments and academia to foster innovation. Prior to that Gina was Vice President of Developer Relations for IBM where she had worldwide responsibility for IBM's developer programs that attract early adopters of technology, individual developers, and independent software vendors to IBM with tools, technical information, education, and interactive on-line resources. She launched and led IBM's developerWorks web community growing it to 8 million members worldwide.

Gina began her career with IBM in 1984 as a programmer in the personal computer division. She has held a number of management positions in IBM's software and hardware divisions including: strategy and operations, technology and industry relationships, product management, and software development. Gina is a certified Project Management Professional (PMP) and holds degrees in computer science, business management, and economics

Philip McKinney

Vice President and CTO, Personal Systems Group,
Hewlett Packard Company

Philip McKinney is HP's Vice President and Chief Technology Officer for the Personal Systems Group (PSG). In this role, he oversees the long-range technical strategy and research and development for HP's laptops, desktops, converged mobile phones, workstations, digital home and consumer media devices.

Prior to his current role, Phil was the Vice President and CTO for HP's Network and Server Provider Business, responsible for the executive CTO relationship, long-range strategy and R&D for HP's largest industry vertical business segment.

Before joining HP, Phil was engaged in the day-to-day operational challenges as the Senior Vice President and founding CIO for Teligent, a global provider of fixed-wireless services. At Teligent, he led the strategy development, IT infrastructure build out and ongoing operations, managing a team of more than 1,000 technology professionals.

Prior to joining Teligent, McKinney was the senior executive responsible for the Communication Industry Consulting Practice at Computer Sciences Corporation (NYSE: CSC) where he directed consulting engagements worldwide. Earlier in his career at CSC, he oversaw the communication industry managed services division that provided mission critical system outsourcing for more than 165 network and service providers worldwide.

McKinney currently serves on the Board of Directors for Signafor, Inc.

Kathy Burke-Thomas

Associate Director, AT&T Project Management Center of Excellence, AT&T

Kathy Burke-Thomas has worked with virtual teams for over 25 years, performing many roles in AT&T's Information Technology and Product Development departments. She joined the AT&T Project Management Center of Excellence at its inception, and now provides services and creates products and training to support the development of project management competency throughout AT&T.

Kathy has earned a bachelor's degree in Business / Computer Science, and an MBA. She is certified by the Project Management Institute as a Project Management Professional. As a Project Manager, she has been responsible for delivering project results through others, typically without the direct supervisory authority provided to the traditional manager. At AT&T, her teams have been located throughout the U.S., and often have not ever met in person.

Kathy has served on the Board of Directors of the Junior League of Wyandotte and Johnson Counties, as the Vice President of Finance and as the Treasurer, and various other leadership roles for approximately 13 years. In these positions she directed organizations made up entirely of volunteers as they carried out at least four major fundraising events per year, and disseminated grants and support funds nearing $500,000 annually.

She has also led a nationally affiliated arts program at the local elementary school for several years, coached girls' soccer, been the "camping mom", and led a record-breaking school fundraiser, all with volunteer committees. She currently is active in playing and promoting the St. Andrew Pipes & Drums band in Kansas City (www. kcpipeband.org).

Lawrence A. McAndrews

CEO, National Association of Childrens Hospitals and Related Institutions (NACHRI)

Lawrence A. McAndrews has become a national spokesman on children's issues and the changing health care marketplace since becoming president and chief executive officer of the National Association of Children's Hospitals and Related Institutions (NACHRI) in September 1992. He also became president and chief executive officer of an independent trade association which is the public policy affiliate of NACHRI, the National Association of Children's Hospitals.

Mr. McAndrews has testified before Congress, met with Executive Branch leaders, been interviewed by print and electronic media, and addressed national conferences on a host of issues involving children's health coverage, graduate medical education, pediatric research and public health protection.

A hospital executive since 1971, Mr. McAndrews was president and chief executive officer at Children's Mercy Hospital in Kansas City, MO, for six years before coming to NACHRI. Mr. McAndrews previously served as administrator of the Prentice Women's Hospital and, before that, of the Institute of Psychiatry—both components of Northwestern Memorial Hospital in Chicago, the teaching site for Northwestern University. Previously, Mr. McAndrews was Vice President/Professional Affairs at Lafayette General Hospital in Lafayette, LA, and administrative assistant at MacNeal Memorial Hospital in Berwyn, IL.

He is the current Vice-Chair of Generations United and is a member of the Coalition to Protect America's Health Care. He served as the past chairman of the Governing Council of the Section for Maternal and Child Health of the American Hospital Association and served on the boards of the Missouri Hospital Association and the Kansas City Area Hospital Association. He also served as a preceptor for the University of Missouri and Northwestern University. Mr. McAndrews is a Fellow of the American College of Health Care Executives.

Mr. McAndrews, 62, holds a Master of Health Administration degree from The George Washington University and a Bachelor's in Psychology from Vanderbilt University. He served two years as an officer in the Army. Mr. McAndrews, a resident of Alexandria, VA, is married and has two adult children.

Jack Barsky

Vice President of Information Technology, NRG

Jack Barsky is the VP of Information Technology at NRG Energy, a $10 billion electric generation company. This role is responsible for all aspects of information technology in the company.

Jack has over 25 years experience in the realm of information technology. He has held management positions at several Fortune 100 companies, such MetLife, United HealthCare, Prudential, and ConEdison Inc. The diverse assignments include Database Administrator, Project Manager, Director of Technology Assessment, Director of Data Center Operations UNIX, Vice President of HR Systems, and Chief Information Officer.

Jack authored a chapter on strategy for the book *Inside the Mind of a CIO/CTO* (Aspatore, 2005). He has given guest lectures at Columbia University and the City University of New York and has spoken at several conferences. He is an active member of the Society for Information Management and a mentor for the Masters in Information Technology program at Columbia University.

Jack graduated as valedictorian with a Bachelor's of Business Administration from Baruch College. He also holds a Master's in Chemistry from the Friedrich Schiller University, Jena Germany.

Piet Hut

Professor of Astrophysics and Head of the Program in Interdisciplinary Studies at the Institute for Advanced Study at Princeton

Piet Hut is currently a professor at the Institute for Advanced Study in Princeton, New Jersey. His main research interest concerns investigations of the structure of the world from different points of view. His work as an astrophysicist aims at increasing our understanding of the physical world on the largest scales of time and space by studying the history of the Universe. Interdisciplinary collaborations have allowed him to branch out from astrophysics per se to physics in general, as well as to geology and paleontology, where he has found each discipline to rely on remarkably different views of the material world. In addition, his research in computer science showed yet other views of the world when seen in the light of structures of information. Over the last several years he has attempted to summarize what he has learned in these various areas through some journeys into natural philosophy.

Acknowledgments

I would like to thank Dick Reilly for his contribution, ongoing collaborations and his friendship. I would also like to thank my husband Paul Lojeski whose editorial skills helped make this book possible. I would also like to extend my sincere thanks to Timothy Burgard, my Managing Editor at Wiley, who continuously offered keen insights, criticism, and direction. So too, I would like to thank Daniel Rasmus, the Managing Editor of the Microsoft Executive Leadership Book Series for his ongoing support and enthusiasm about this work. I would also like to thank David Ferguson, the Chairman of the Department of Technology and Society at Stony Brook University. Dave has given me the time and resources needed to continue my research and writing in the best of all possible work environments and for that I am sincerely appreciative. I would also like to thank the many executives and thought-leaders who spent time in interviews and other electronic discussions that ultimately made their way into the development of the ideas discussed in this book. Their detailed accounts of what works and what doesn't for leaders in today's digital age are what make this book unique and unlike any other leadership books that have come before it. And for this I am sincerely grateful. Included in this group are Steven A. Tainer, Robert McMahon, Cheri Sterman, Guido Petit, Gina Poole, Philip McKinney, Kathy Burke-Thomas, Lawrence A. McAndrews, Jack Barsky, Piet Hut, and Jessica Lipnack. I would also like to thank all of my dear friends and colleagues who continue to embrace and expound the importance of understanding and dealing with Virtual Distance. Their continued evangelism and support keep me motivated to push further each and every day.

CHAPTER 1

A Whole New World

World markets are unsteady, unemployment is on the rise, housing foreclosures are up, asset values are down, and the political landscape is shifting.

Under such tumultuous conditions people often look to leaders to soothe battered nerves and listen for reassurances portending better days. But in today's rough and tumble environment, there are reportedly few leaders the average person relies upon.

A GROWING LEADERSHIP CRISIS

According to a recent study, 80 percent of Americans believe there is a major leadership crisis across many industry sectors with only two exceptions; leaders in the military and in medicine still rank relatively high. However, confidence in business leaders fell more than in any other area, including the highly unpopular government sector.[1]

Globally, the crisis of leadership is also taking a heavy toll. IBM reported "companies are heading toward a perfect storm when it comes to leadership," according to Eric Lesser who led the study. IBM surveyed 400 human resources executives from 40 different countries. In the Asia-Pacific region, 88 percent of companies reported concern over their ability to develop future leaders with about 75 percent reporting the same in Latin America, Europe, the Middle East, and Africa, as well as 69 percent in North America.[2]

The growing leadership crisis did not develop overnight. In fact after World War II, optimism, trust, and support for American business leadership soared. Harvard Business School Professor and *BusinessWeek* writer Shoshanna Zuboff reported that in the mid-1950s, 80 percent of U.S. adults said that "Big Business" was a good thing for the country and 76 percent believed that business required little or no change. By 1966, that number had skidded to 55 percent of Americans who held a high degree of confidence in big company leaders. And by 2006, business leaders' good will had, for the most part, evaporated. According to a Zogby poll taken that same year, only 7 percent of Americans had a high level of trust in corporate leaders.

It took over half a century for leadership support to sink. But declining trust for executives is not the only trend wreaking havoc with the workforce populace. A completely different organizational landscape has been carved out of the relatively staid and bureaucratic structures of earlier eras. Leaps in technology and its use in global business are at the heart of this colossal shift.

A CHANGED WORKFORCE

The speed and pace at which technology has forever changed the way we work, with whom, where, when, and how, is practically unfathomable. Out of all recent information and communication technology (ICT), the Internet outpaced all of its predecessors in reaching critical mass. To reach 50 million users it took:

- 75 years for the telephone
- 38 years for the radio

- 17 years for the television
- 11 years for the personal computer

However, it took only 3 years for the Internet to reach over 50 million users, as Figure 1.2 illustrates.

IBM's Global Human Capital Study identified some of the most important critical success factors to developing an adaptable workforce. The top three highlighted were:

1. The ability to predict future skills
   - Successfully anticipating future business scenarios enables organizations to know what key competencies to target in advance of critical market shifts.
   - Only 13 percent of organizations interviewed believe they have a very clear understanding of the skills they will require in the next three to five years.
2. The ability to locate experts
   - While predicting future skills is important, so is the ability to apply existing knowledge and skills to new challenges.
   - Expertise location is cited by respondents as critical in identifying and allocating resources to address new opportunities and threats.
   - Only 13 percent believe they are very capable of identifying individuals with specific expertise within the organization.
   - Companies are using a variety of techniques to improve their expertise location capability.
   - More than 50 percent of companies that rate themselves as "very effective" in locating experts use some form of employee directory while only 39 percent of all respondents report using them.
3. The ability to foster collaboration
   - Once the experts are located and identified, collaboration is the next step to foster innovation and growth.
   - According to the study, only 8 percent of companies believe they are very effective in fostering collaboration across the enterprise.
   - Surprisingly, technology is not the deterrent to effective collaboration, with only 28 percent of companies indicating this is a significant factor.
   - Instead, organizational silos (42 percent) are the leading barrier of collaboration in an organization, followed by time pressures (40 percent) and misaligned performance measures (39 percent).

FIGURE 1.1   More Startling Stats

Source: IBM Global Human Capital Study: "Looming Leadership Crisis, Organizations Placing Their Companies' Growth Strategies at Risk." www-03.ibm.com/press/us/en/pressrelease/22471.wss

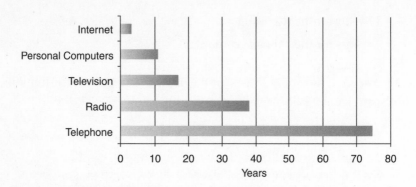

FIGURE 1.2   Number of Years to Reach 50 Million Users

Source: Adapted from numbers presented in William McGaughey, *Five Epochs of Civilization: World History as Emerging in Five Civilizations* (Minneapolis, MN: Thistlerose Publications, 2000).

With the commercial availability of the Internet via browser technology loaded on to every new PC and smartphone rolling off the assembly line, coupled with faster, cheaper, and better access to high-speed telecommunications, came significant corporate leverage of resources. Organizational leaders realized that people could work more efficiently and be free from physical location limitations. This led to higher management expectations of productivity that dovetailed increasingly elevated levels of technological skill across a wide swath of corporate foot soldiers. Not only did applications like spreadsheets and word processors quicken the pace of what had been manually intensive work, but when paired with anytime, anywhere Internet access, people were able to do more work longer.

Then came miniaturization. This led to the development of portable laptops, PDAs, and other intelligent computing devices that fit in the palm of a hand. And businesses took advantage. Many soon realized they could tap into mobile labor pools all over the world. In fact, the mobile workforce is rising dramatically. According to the International Data Corporation (IDC), the mobile workforce will increase from about 768 million, or 24.8 percent of the global workforce, to over 1 billion, representing 30.4 percent of worldwide workers by 2011. The largest percentage of mobile workers is in the United States, which had 68 percent in 2006, and is predicted to grow to 73 percent by 2011. Asia/Pacific (excluding Japan) will have the largest number of mobile workers. The region had 480 million mobile workers in 2006, and that number will grow to reach 671 million in 2011—that's more mobile workers in the region than the Unites States has population!

Substitute the word "mobile" as described by IDC, with the word "virtual," and you end up with the workforce at the center of this book.

In addition to having unfettered, unbounded access to the virtual workforce, organizations found that labor costs were significantly cheaper outside and it became financially irresistible to increase the use of resources located in countries where pay scales were sometimes a fraction of U.S. wage standards.

The financial impetus to push performance levels ever higher using the newly equipped virtual workforce soon surfaced a glaring need; to change the way organizations were structured. Most organizations today are derivatives of the "vertical" structure. Vertically integrated enterprises are those that are tightly held together from top to bottom using strong, formal hierarchies. In a traditional vertical design all functions reside within the boundaries of the organization. For example, the Human Resources department employs people who work directly for the organization they support. Manufacturing is staffed with people who produce the product the company makes. Sales are made by people who work for the company that produces the goods and whose benefits are managed by the Human Resources department within the same company. In sum, the vertical organization houses everyone needed to produce goods and services as well as support customers and staff.

However, the notion of vertical organizations seems almost quaint, like antique furniture staged in an old farmhouse on display for those who have never been near dairy cows. With competitive closeness and cost constraints tightening rapidly, vertical institutions have gone the way of the dinosaur—in reality they have become extinct. Organizational charts and management theories used to describe them are like fossils—relic imprints of organisms long gone. And yet many of today's most trusted management strategies ironically rely on these petrified frames. This begs the question: Do they still work as designed and should leaders use them as the best way to build lasting success? Figure 1.4 considers these questions.

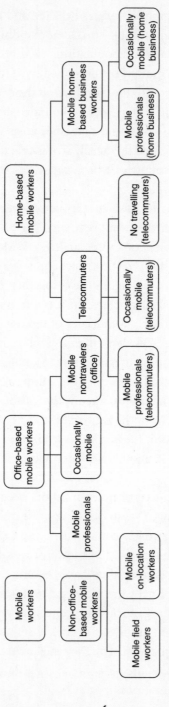

FIGURE 1.3   The IDC Workforce Hierarchy

Source: Adapted from IDC, 2008

Consider for a moment the seminal work of Michael Porter, *Competitive Advantage*, a must-read for any self-respecting MBA student. Porter describes three main strategies to competitive victory: Cost Leadership, Differentiation, and Focus. Using the Cost Leadership strategy, organizations try to establish themselves as the lowest cost producer of goods or services. In the Differentiation strategy, organizations try to build unique value across a broad market segment. And in the Focus strategy, organizations target a narrower segment using either Cost Leadership or Differentiation.

Porter espoused that executing competitive strategies successfully required resources with specific skill sets against the backdrop of particular organizational elements. For example, in the Cost Leadership strategy, "intense supervision of resources" is required along with "highly structured organizations and responsibilities." But today's modern executive wants little to do with close supervision of anyone. As a matter of fact, many cost-cutting strategies rely upon flattening the organization, allowing people to work from anywhere, shedding real estate as well as management layers to streamline operations. Organizations and their underlying structure change rapidly these days. Therefore any attempt to enforce discrete divisional definitions or territorial margins is likely to fail.

In Porter's Differentiation strategy, leaders are guided to look for people with "creative flair" and pay them on the basis of "subjective measurement and incentives that are not quantitatively based." Of course anyone who has been in the workforce for any given amount of time knows that performance metrics in the twenty-first century are based almost exclusively on hard numbers—exactly when and how much of something is delivered. Can you imagine going to a conference offering a track entitled, "Subjective, Qualitative Incentives: The Key to Innovation and Profit"? Not one manager we know would spend precious financial resource to send anyone to that one. And yet we still expect Cost Leadership and Differentiation strategies, as originally designed and currently taught, to work in today's marketplace.

FIGURE 1.4   What Does Competitive Advantage Mean Today?
Source: Adapted from Michael E. Porter, *Competitive Advantage: Creating and Sustaining Superior Performance*, (New York: Free Press, 1998)

While bits of competitive advantage and other management theories are still episodically applicable their essence feels a little like the man behind the curtain in the *Wizard of Oz*; obscure, antiquated, and in denial. Tried and true they might be; however, inherently these models are based on assumptions that have long since perished.

In his 2006 *Foreign Affairs* article, Sam Palmisano, Chairman and CEO of IBM, talked about the pressing need for executives to let go of dated conceptualizations of business structures.

Many parties to the globalization debate mistakenly project into the future a picture of corporations that is unchanged from that of today or yesterday. This happens as often among free-market advocates as it does among people opposed to globalization. But businesses are changing in fundamental ways—structurally, operationally, culturally—in response to the imperatives of globalization and new technology. As CEO and chair of the board of IBM, I have observed this within IBM and among our clients. And I believe that rather than continuing to focus on past models, regulators, scholars, nongovernmental organizations, community leaders, and business executives would be best served by thinking about the global corporation of the future and its implications for new approaches to regulation, education, trade, and commerce.

—Excerpt from Samuel J. Palmisano, "The Globally Integrated Enterprise," *Foreign Affairs*, (May/June 2006), 127 [Vol. 85 No. 3]

The structures that many still adhere to belong to an era past; a time when vertical organizations were locked into place in the early part of the twentieth century, guided by gurus like Frederick Winslow Taylor who espoused one-to-one reporting in a top-down closely knit structure with management at the top overseeing the unskilled workers at the bottom. Lattices like these provided the foundation upon which long-term competitive strategies were developed in the context of a market where there still shone a bit of patience; a sense of time and scale about what it would take to bring a product to market and diffuse to the point where the company could claim cornering. But all of that has changed.

Institutional frameworks have morphed into what look more like pancakes; flat, lumpy, and a bit overdone around the edges. They are fueled by highly skilled, specially trained knowledge workers, spread out, communicating side to side, and at the fringe, consist of contractors and other malleable resources that carry no fixed costs and are easily disposed of when belt-tightening is needed. Even so, ask a typical person to draw a picture of their organization and most often they will render a traditional top-down org chart, representing formal hierarchies and reporting relationships. While pictograms of this sort are helpful in seeing who's who, they no longer represent the relationships that really matter. So organizations are suffering an identity crisis as well as a leadership crisis.

VIRTUAL WORKFORCE DYNAMICS

While massive shifts in organizational structure occur at the macro level, workers are shuffled around much like the ball in a street shell game. With laptops and smartphones in hand, the traditional worker has been downsized, outsourced, right-sized; swept up by the latest merger and assigned a new affiliation or divorced completely from corporate relationships only to re-emerge as an entrepreneur or self-employed consultant hired by the same company. This type of organization looks much more like a network; a network of people linked together by binding ties like deliverables and project assignments, regardless of organizational affiliation. But many still try and shove individuals into boxes on a fossilized diagram with all the performance expectations that come along with tightly integrated formal management processes and assume people will carry out edicts as described by Taylor and others. This view presupposes that because we have really "nifty" collaboration technology it will all "come together at the end of the day." Yet it doesn't.

When leaders use old management models to try and solve new challenges *and*, at the same time expect individuals in social networks, tied together by electronic gadgetry, to behave exactly the same way as they did when grouped next to each other in offices where the organizational chart truly represented the working hierarchy, phantom expectations of leader effectiveness and worker performance emerge and usually miss the mark. The reason—the rise of Virtual Distance.

The Rise of Virtual Distance

The higher one goes in an organization, the more tempting it is to hang on to outdated frameworks, because, let's face it, they're straightforward and easy for everyone to understand. And for all the talk and endless books that decree social networks, crowd-sourcing, and unimagined creative powers being unleashed by the worldwide web, generally speaking, experience tells us that organizations have not been able to effectively describe or implement leadership models or performance standards that take advantage of this vast virtual array. The more the new virtual workforce is managed using obsolete models, the more performance and innovation degrades.

As this mismatching continues, new phenomena appear. They show up as unintended consequences or "revenge effects" like those Edward Tenner described in his book, *Why Things Bite Back: Technology and the Revenge of Unintended Consequences.*[3] Revenge effects are the detrimental and unplanned byproducts resulting from the introduction of technology in one form or another. To combat them one has to first admit they exist and, second seek out and detect them.

One of the revenge effects of ubiquitous communication technology and the expansion of the virtual workforce, introduced under the auspices of vertical vestiges was detailed in the predecessor to this book entitled, *Uniting the Virtual Workforce: Transforming Leadership and Innovation in the Globally Integrated Enterprise.*[4] The newly discovered phenomenon was called *Virtual Distance.*

To summarize, Virtual Distance is a perceived distance that gets bigger and bigger as people rely more and more on communication technology like e-mail, IM, avatars, and so on. The most important aspects of Virtual Distance are that it can be measured, predicted, and when it is high, can have significant and negative consequences to the organization. As Figure 1.5 shows, as Virtual Distance increases critical success factors decline significantly.

When Virtual Distance is relatively high, individuals and groups unconsciously grow to feel or experience others as being far away. And here's something that at first was surprising but quickly became obvious: Virtual Distance exists in many instances among people who sit right next door to each other as well as between geographically dispersed individuals and teams.

Collaboration technology, meant to help people feel closer to colleagues and peers, is of no use when Virtual Distance is high. Virtual Distance not only prevents that from happening, it can exacerbate both real and perceived differences between individuals, groups, and organizations. In addition, when Virtual Distance is high, leader performance is perceived as relatively low. To say it another way, when Virtual Distance is high it creates low trust or in many cases distrust, blurriness

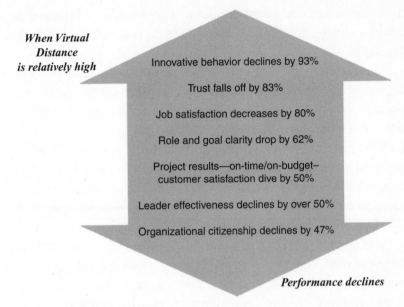

When Virtual Distance is relatively high

Innovative behavior declines by 93%

Trust falls off by 83%

Job satisfaction decreases by 80%

Role and goal clarity drop by 62%

Project results—on-time/on-budget—customer satisfaction dive by 50%

Leader effectiveness declines by over 50%

Organizational citizenship declines by 47%

Performance declines

FIGURE 1.5   When Virtual Distance is High, Performance Declines

about roles and goals, and significantly less citizenship behaviors like helping fellow workers when it calls for extra time and effort outside of the normal job. When these dynamics are set in motion, perceptions of the leader's effectiveness also take a dive.

Despite some popular views that a "leaderless" business organization can be a workable reality or that somehow "newly empowered" people will simply figure things out on their own, good leaders remain crucial to organizational networks. Some argue that it's possible to run organizations without any "organization." In *Here Comes Everybody: The Power of Organizing without Organizations*,[5] Clay Shirky uses colorful examples of how ubiquitous access to the web has resulted in some astounding social movements. He argues that Web 2.0, wikis, blogs, and other digital developments are revolutionizing the social order. But so far our bouillabaisse of change includes a growing worldwide leadership crisis, mounting organizational identity crises, and big blows to performance and innovation brought on by increasingly high levels of high Virtual Distance. Just because anyone can get on the Internet and in certain settings rally people to act in impressive ways for social and political change, doesn't really change the pecking order in which they live day to day.

Paul Saffo is a well-known technology futurist. He likes to say that "it takes 20 years to become an overnight success."[6] Similarly, in his book *Outliers*[7] Malcolm Gladwell dispels the myth that people like Bill Gates and other superstar greats like Mozart had such special gifts they leap-frogged their contemporaries and rose to the top by virtue of pure genius alone. Instead Gladwell shows that it takes at least 10,000 hours or about 10 years of intense work and practice before a star is born. Do some get lucky? Of course. And luck plays a big part in the lives of those who have clocked the time as well.

So while the temptation is there to buy in completely to the notion that a finely crafted "blogpost" or "wiki" is going to suddenly change much in the long run, it's a dangerous and slippery slope. And when this fantasy gets transmogrified into the widespread dogma that enabling new social networks through technology alone is going to instantaneously create well-oiled, productive, and profitable workforces, companies fail. While it may seem that everyone out there suddenly and miraculously has the power to move mountains, it is in part yet another myth being shaped by digital dynamos.

The fact of the matter is that effective leaders are desperately needed; as demonstrated by the vast number of people around the world who report worry about the future in light of a growing leadership vacuum. They are needed because hierarchy dynamics based on power and status, as well as attention and recognition, emerge just as readily in cyberspace as they do in office space—human nature goes unchanged.

> The lapse of ages changes all things—time, language, the earth, the bounds of the sea, the stars of the sky, and everything "about, around, and underneath" man, except man himself.
> —Lord Byron (1788–1824), British Poet

Leaders are needed to positively affect change and advancement while overseeing and ridding the organization of nonproductive behaviors that can quickly become destructive to fiber-based teams. Therefore, today's leaders need to be concerned with not only the usual suspects of performance and team-building, they also need to be aware of invisible online politics and other human tendencies that can preclude progressive achievement, and instead, stoke the flames of innovation and cooperation in a complexly interwoven world. All the while, leaders must also remain fully grounded in the reality that people are people and will behave in ways that are both positive and negative to gain power and control in whatever form, adventurous or social, to which they are inclined.

A crisis is only dubbed as such if there is a breakdown in something that's needed; a rapid deterioration of shared values and respected exemplars. Growing Virtual Distance between leader and follower in part fuels the leadership crisis that has arisen worldwide. In addition a perceived lack of respect for human beings in general has grown. There are some leaders who unrealistically apply fantastical and magical powers to the underlying inert virtual communication technology. They espouse the virtues of non–face-to-face encounters using words that unintentionally yet determinately deconstruct and disrespect the human being. John Schwartz, the leader of Sun Microsystems, dubs in-person encounters as "flesh meetings" and blogs about how wonderful it is to avoid all that comes along with such woefully "overrated" interactions.[8] At *Fortune* magazine's 2008 Brainstorm conference, technology leaders incessantly used the word "eyeballs" to describe the main feature of their customer base. And yet, leaders at Google, the world leader in providing virtual content and information, believe that people work best when seated together side by side. Google managers insist that employees come into an office each day and stay there as long as possible—using free food, concierge services, day care, healthcare treatment and other incentives to do so.

While terms like "flesh meetings" and "eyeballs" used to describe human contact and relationships may sound harmless enough in isolation, when taken on as widely-used cultural euphemisms they become eminently powerful and inherently intimate certain kinds of behavior that runs counter to virtual workforce leader expectations. As technology changes everything about the way in which people work it actually changes very little when it comes to social dynamics. People still need authoritative role models and trustworthy organizers to mold and configure the organizational structure in ways that complement new skills and situations enabled by virtual workspaces. But that's not all. The workforce also needs leaders who demonstrate fairness across electronic workspaces; who seek out new ways to show they are not only in charge, but also care about all. It is these most fundamental and cherished leader attributes that have always been the main motivators of healthy human behavior.

The Need for New Models

To overcome the leadership and organizational identity crisis now subsuming many organizations, original ideas about how best to nurture the global workforce need to come to light as soon as possible. In this book, we take one step toward illuminating a new kind of leader to achieve that goal. We name this person the **Virtual Distance Leader**.

The executives and other thought leaders selected and studied for this book all have the requisite skills, abilities, and intuitive powers needed for this enormous challenge. They represent authoritative figures that wield power and influence with others yet mindfully step out of old management paradigms and find new ways to motivate the human spirit. They embody varied industries and areas of expertise. What sets them apart is their meta-cognitive abilities; their willingness to look beyond themselves and what has worked in the past, to forge new ways forward. These and other luminaries demonstrate that the **Virtual Distance Leader** maintains an open mind and a sense of wonder about their cyber-based surroundings and finds ways to enliven and unite those that populate them. The leaders showcased in this work express authentic caring and responsibility for those who depend upon them. But most of all they demonstrate respect toward their fellow human beings, an all-too-frequent casualty of our time.

NOTES

1. S.A. Rosenthal, T.L. Pittinsky, S. Moore, J.J. Ratcliff, L.A. Maruskin, and C.A. Gravelin, "National Leadership Index 2008," Center for Public Leadership at Harvard University's Kennedy School of Government and the Merriman River Group.

2. IBM Global Human Capital Study: "Looming Leadership Crisis, Organizations Placing Their Companies' Growth Strategies at Risk." www-03.ibm.com/press/us/en/pressrelease/22471.wss

3. E. Tenner, *Why Things Bite Back: Technology and the Revenge of Unintended Consequences* (New York: Alfred A. Knopf, 1996).

4. K. Sobel Lojeski and R. Reilly, *Uniting the Virtual Workforce: Transforming Leadership and Innovation in the Globally Integrated Enterprise* (Hoboken, NJ: John Wiley & Sons, 2008).

5. C. Shirky, *Here Comes Everybody: The Power of Organizing without Organizations* (New York: Penguin Group, 2008).

6. Comments made by Paul Saffo in July, 2007 at a dinner reception during the Stanford Summer Institute led by Charles House, Executive Director, Stanford MediaX Lab.

7. M. Gladwell, *Outliers* (New York: Little Brown & Company, 2008).

8. "Labor Movement: The Joys and Drawbacks of Being Able to Work Anywhere," *The Economist* (2008) www.economist.com/specialreports/displaystory.cfm?STORY_ID=10950378

CHAPTER **2**

A Brief History of Leadership

S hakespeare's sixteenth century play, *Twelfth Night*, nicely describes three of the dominant approaches to the study of leadership in the twentieth century:

> Be not afraid of greatness: some are born great, some achieve greatness and some have greatness thrust upon them.
> —Act II, Scene V, *Twelfth Night* by W. Shakespeare

Trait models assume that leaders are born to greatness, *behavioral models* assume that individuals can become great leaders through their efforts and *contingency models* assume that great leaders have greatness thrust upon them by the situation. These are all illustrated in Figure 2.1.

Given that these are the most popular and well researched leadership models, let's take a look at each of these, and two lesser known leader frameworks, to better understand their implications for leading the virtual workforce.

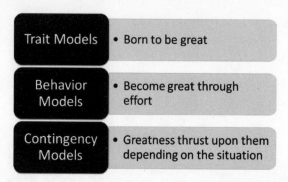

FIGURE 2.1   Three Dominant Approaches to the Study of Leadership in the 20th Century

TRAIT MODELS OF LEADERSHIP

Think about how you describe people you know. Odds are that you think about them in terms of traits. "She is an extravert" and "he is neurotic" are examples of trait descriptions. Traits are the characteristics that make us distinguishable from one another. Traits include needs, motives, and personality factors. The notion of human traits can be traced back to the work of Francis Galton, a cousin of Charles Darwin. Galton was interested in exploring the role of heredity on behavior, which led him to develop a series of tests and questionnaires to measure mental abilities and other traits.[1] Galton's work led to the development of psychological measurements of intelligence and other abilities as well as personality and related traits.

Later, psychologists became interested in determining whether leaders could be identified by certain traits. They were interested in whether there are "born leaders" who could be distinguished by certain behavioral traits, or consistent patterns of behavior. In the 1960s David McClelland, a Harvard psychologist, led one of the earliest research programs on leadership traits by examining what he called "needs." More specifically, McClelland studied several needs that were thought to be important for leadership:

- Individuals with a high *need for achievement* derive satisfaction from task accomplishment and demonstrating excellence.

- Those with a high *need for affiliation* are concerned with being liked, accepted, and enjoy social interaction, as well as collaboration with friends and coworkers.
- McClelland also studied the *need for power* and discovered that there are two types of power: socialized power and personalized power.
  - Those with a high need for socialized power derive satisfaction from influencing others to achieve something worthwhile or helping to develop others.
  - Those with a high need for personalized power enjoy dominating others and using power to satisfy their own desires.

McClelland found that successful leaders tend to have a moderately high need for achievement, a high need for socialized power, and a low need for affiliation—ironically the need most satisfied by virtual communication technology.

Case One: David McClelland and the Magic Mushrooms

David McClelland was one of the most influential and respected psychologists of the twentieth century. But his work might have taken a different turn if not for a Mexican cook. McClelland, who was the Director of Harvard's Center for Personality Research, spent the summer of 1960 in Tepoztlan, Mexico working on his book, *The Achieving Society*. In that same summer, a Harvard colleague whom McClelland had recently hired was also spending the summer in nearby Cuernevaca. Timothy Leary was the colleague. After his first experience with psychedelic mushrooms that summer he invited McClelland to visit him and do mushrooms with him. As McClelland tells it, "He was very excited because some Mexican curandero had given him the magic mushroom and he had taken it and had this marvelous experience. And he invited us to come over and take them too. I didn't much want to but my wife did. She was an artist and intrigued to see what would happen

(continued)

to her. So we drove over to his house in Cuernevaca, but unfortunately the cook had cooked the mushrooms. Or fortunately, from my point of view. So I wasn't faced with the decision to take them or not." Leary, of course, later became infamous as a counterculture icon and for his advocacy of psychedelic drugs, especially LSD. McClelland went on to develop his ideas about leadership and how traits such as the need for achievement and the need for socialized power play a major role.

Source: Robert Greenfield, *Timothy Leary: A Biography* (New York: Harcourt, 2006.)

Personality factors represent another important area of leadership. So how do leaders stack up on personality? Research has produced a large number of different theories and models of personality that in the past made it difficult to understand how personality is related to leadership. Fortunately, more recent developments make things a bit easier. Several researchers have used sophisticated mathematical and statistical techniques to examine the many different ways that personality can be described. Their results have consistently shown that there are five broad categories of personality and that the same categories consistently describe personality across many different cultures.[2] Sometimes referred to as the "Big Five" the factors include Extraversion, Neuroticism, Conscientiousness, Agreeableness, and Openness.

The two most important personality factors for traditional leadership are Extraversion (positive) and Neuroticism (negative). Extraverts tend to be assertive, active, optimistic, talkative, and upbeat. Extraversion has some overlap with McClelland's need for social power. Neuroticism, on the other hand, is not a good attribute for leaders to have. Neuroticism is characterized by negative emotions such as fear, sadness, guilt, and anger.

In face-to-face settings the importance of each of these characteristics makes sense. Although these two factors are the most highly related[3] to traditional notions of leadership the other personality factors might actually be more important for leading virtual teams. Agreeableness is the tendency to be cooperative and trusting—two qualities that are extremely important for working with others virtually. Agreeableness, which has some overlap with McClelland's need for affiliation, describes individuals who tend to be trusting and more willing to share leadership with others, which is an important factor in managing a virtual team where members are dispersed around the world. Openness includes intellectual curiosity, flexibility in attitudes, and imagination—all traits that might be important for leading a diverse group of individuals differing in culture and background. Highly open leaders are more likely to be able to take the perspective of members from other cultures and appreciate the context within which diverse members are operating. Openness in leaders has also been found to be important on tasks involving new or radical innovations.[4] Conscientiousness, which has some overlap with McClelland's need for achievement, includes working hard towards goals, the tendency to be well organized and disciplined—characteristics that are important for leader of virtual projects where individuals may be working on multiple tasks and communicating asynchronously.

CONTINGENCY MODELS OF LEADERSHIP

When Shakespeare said, "Some have greatness thrust upon them" he could have been describing contingency models of leadership. Contingency models exemplify the view that an individual may be an effective leader depending upon the situation. An example is Winston Churchill, who was a great leader during World War II but an ineffective and unsuccessful one before and after the war. Although there are several contingency models they all have in common this notion of the situation being the key factor in determining whether a particular style of leadership will be effective. One of the best-known contingency models is the Path-Goal Theory of leadership.[5] According to this theory there are four different styles of leaders:

1. *Supportive Leaders* give consideration to the needs of subordinates, display concern for their welfare, and create a friendly climate.

2. *Directive Leaders* let subordinates know what they are expected to do, give specific guidance, schedule work, and ask subordinates to follow rules and procedures.

3. *Participative Leaders* consult with subordinates and take their opinions as well as suggestions into account.

4. *Achievement-Oriented Leaders* set challenging goals, seek performance improvements, emphasize excellence, and show confidence that subordinates will perform effectively.

As Table 2.1 shows, different leadership styles will be more or less effective depending upon the kinds of tasks and the kinds of subordinates involved. For example, a highly directive leader will probably not be successful with an experienced team working on improvements to an existing product. The team is competent and the task is highly structured. A directive leader might be perceived as micromanaging and taking up time with unnecessary activities. It should be noted that contingency models were developed before the widespread use of virtual teams. Although the kinds of situations described can certainly exist with virtual teams, most virtual teams have additional characteristics not envisioned by the proponents of contingency models and there is little research to help understand how these models might work with virtual, global teams.

TABLE 2.1   Path-Goal Leadership Styles

Leadership Style	Is Most Effective When	Is Least Effective When
Supportive	Tasks are boring, tedious, or dangerous	Tasks are interesting and enjoyable
Directive	Tasks are unstructured and complex, and subordinates are inexperienced, and roles are ambiguous	Tasks are structured and/or subordinates are highly competent
Participative	Tasks are unstructured and subordinates have high need for achievement and autonomy	Tasks are structured and subordinates have low need for achievement and autonomy
Achievement Oriented	Tasks are complex and nonrepetitive	Tasks are simple and repetitive

BEHAVIORAL MODELS OF LEADERSHIP

Behavioral models incorporate several different approaches to leadership including **transactional**, **charismatic**, and **transformational** leadership.

Transactional Leadership

Perhaps the most traditional view of leadership is transactional. A transactional leader is essentially a manager: one who monitors, controls, and, most importantly, rewards desired behavior and punishes undesired behavior. Transactional leaders view their relationship with employees as an implicit contract to accomplish specified tasks for specific rewards. Work is viewed as a series of transactions. I will reward you with something you want (e.g., money) if you do what I ask you to do. Transactional leaders can be active: setting goals, constantly monitoring employees, and meting out rewards or punishment; this is called Contingent Reward.

Or leaders can be more passive. The passive approach is sometimes called Management by Exception. These managers wait until a positive or negative behavior occurs and then reward or punish the behavior. Two books originally published in the 1980s exemplify the principles of the transactional model. *The One Minute Manager*[6] recommends three keys to good management:

1. Setting clear and specific goals
2. Rewarding or praising desired behavior
3. Reprimanding or punishing undesired behavior

The amusing book, *Leadership Secrets of Attila the Hun*[7] has Attila imparting his wisdom in the form of a transactional leadership model. For example, Attila discusses setting goals and expectations as follows:

> Chieftains must teach their Huns well that which is expected of them. Otherwise, Huns will probably do something not expected of them.[8]

Attila also recognized the importance of rewarding followers for desired behavior:

Be generous with small tokens of appreciation-they will multiply in returned loyalty and service.[9]

Is transactional leadership effective? The answer based on the research is yes, *if* the focus is on productivity.[10] But most scholars make a big distinction between management and leadership. Even though the transactional model can be an effective way to manage, most experts see leadership as something more than a series of transactions. True leadership involves an emotional connection with followers, which can be created differently depending on the style of leadership. Two views of leadership that emphasize this emotional connection are charismatic leadership and transformational leadership.

Charismatic Leadership

In 1930 Mohandas Gandhi, who was then 60 years old, began walking the almost 250 miles from his Ashram to the sea in Dandi, Gujarat to protest the British salt tax.[11] Thousands of Indians joined Gandhi on his march despite the threat of imprisonment by the British. The Salt March, as it became known, was just one of many extraordinary acts in the life of Gandhi that led eventually to the independence of India from Great Britain.

Gandhi possessed all of the characteristics of a charismatic leader. First, he articulated a compelling vision, that of a free and self-sufficient India. Second, he served as a behavioral model for his followers. Gandhi lived simply and was often photographed at his spinning wheel, the symbol of independence from British textiles. He inspired a high level of commitment and confidence among his followers as demonstrated by their adherence to his policy of nonviolent resistance. Third, Gandhi was courageous in challenging the British Raj and spent long years in prison as a result. Finally, Gandhi's behavior was very different from most leaders. The Salt March is one of many examples of unconventional behavior that helped to form an emotional connection between Gandhi and the Indian people.

The notion of charismatic leadership comes originally from the work of Max Weber, a sociologist, who used the term charismatic to differentiate political or social leadership that is not based on formal authority but on the idea that the leader is an extraordinary person. The charismatic leadership model has been taken out of the political realm and applied to the business world by researchers such as Robert House[12] and others. There has been a fair amount of scholarship devoted to charismatic leadership. Some of the positive aspects of charismatic leadership, such as inspiring high levels of commitment, can be an asset. But the consensus on charismatic leadership is that it's a mixed bag. Although such leaders can attract incredibly devoted followers, they also tend to be divisive and can even be destructive, as the history of the twentieth century has shown us with leaders such as Hitler and Mao. Charismatic leaders depend on a strong emotional connection with their followers, which in virtual organizations can be difficult to create and sustain over time. It's not clear whether charismatic leadership is possible or even relevant in the virtual enterprise.

Transformational Leadership

Probably the most popular model of leadership in recent years has been Transformational Leadership. Transformational leaders have four characteristics:

1. *Ideal influence:* This is done by serving as a model through their own behavior. This ideal influence creates a strong identification with the leader among followers.

2. *Individual consideration:* By genuinely caring for their followers and promoting feelings of self-efficacy—convincing followers that they can be successful.

3. *Inspirational motivation:* They articulate a clear, compelling vision, which results in inspirational motivation and helps the team move toward its goals.

4. *Intellectual stimulation*: They are able to provide this by presenting new ideas and acting as a change agent as well as also bringing individual followers into developing solutions.

There is some overlap between transformational leadership and charismatic leadership. Idealized influence and compelling visions are charismatic attributes of transformational leaders. However, the organizationally based charisma displayed by transformational leaders has been referred to as a "tamer" version of the revolutionary charisma possessed by leaders such as Gandhi and Mao.

All of these models have something useful to tell us about leadership but all were developed with the notion of a leader in close proximity to followers in a world that emphasized face-to-face communication and where people were not connected digitally and globally.

Two lesser known-models, servant leadership and authentic leadership, may have more relevance to leading in the virtual age.

SERVANT LEADERSHIP

Robert K. Greenleaf was an executive for many years at AT&T, retiring in 1964. His 40 years of corporate experience left him dissatisfied with traditional approaches to leadership that he felt were authoritarian and highly power based. As Greenleaf says, "this story clearly says that the great leader is seen as a servant first and that simple fact is the key to his greatness."[13]

Perhaps the single most important element of Servant Leadership is the notion that true leadership can only be granted by followers when they recognize that the leader is acting as a servant to the needs and motivations of those being led. The behavior of servant leaders includes such characteristics as listening, empathy, persuasion, stewardship, commitment to the growth of people, and building community.

Greenleaf's ideas found support among religious and charitable institutions where volunteers serve as followers but had little impact on mainstream leadership thinking. However, some of the elements of servant leadership are highly relevant to leading virtual enterprises. Virtual teams, for example, are often made up of individuals who serve on multiple projects and leaders must, of necessity, lead without formal authority or status. The executives and thought-leaders interviewed for this book said that, across the board, virtual teams function more effectively when leadership is conferred not by role or authority but by the contribution that individuals make on behalf of the team's mission.

Case Two: Herman Hesse's Servant Leader

In 1932 Herman Hesse published a short novel with the German Title, *Die Morgenlandfahrt* which became known in English as *Journey to the East*. The novel tells the story of a group of people, both historical and fictional, who belong to a society called The Order. Mozart, Plato, Don Quixote, and Hesse himself (thinly disguised as the narrator) join with others on a difficult journey to the "East" in search of the ultimate truth. One of the more interesting aspects of this work is that it reflects many of the aspects of Virtual Distance—differences in culture, geography, time, and space. One other member of the group is a simple servant, Leo, a pleasant, happy person who seems to enjoy a rapport with all of the members of the disparate characters. The journey goes smoothly until one day Leo disappears and the group becomes unable to function effectively. As a result the mission is a failure. Later, the narrator discovers that Leo was actually the leader of the Order and he had disappeared as a test of the group's faith. Leo was a literary example of a servant leader.

You might be thinking that servant leadership sounds nice but can it really work in the real, competitive world of business? The answer is yes. Southwest Airlines has been by many accounts the most successful airline in the United States for the past 25 years.[14] Much of the credit for Southwest's success is given to Herb Kelleher who was the CEO of Southwest for most of that time. Here is what Kelleher had to say about leadership in 1997.

> We are not looking for blind obedience. We are looking for people who, on their own initiative, want to be doing what they are doing because they consider it a worthy objective. I have always believed that the best

leader is the best server. And if you're a servant, by definition, you're not controlling.[15]

Case Three: Buddhism and Leadership

Steven A. Tainer has studied Eastern contemplative traditions intensively since 1970 with many Tibetan, Chinese, and Korean masters. After practicing for a number of years in both mountain retreats and ordinary life circumstances, he now teaches Buddhist, Taoist, and Confucian fundamentals. His specialties are Indian Buddhist philosophy, the "Unity of the Three Traditions" in Chinese thought, Taoist yogic practice, and Ch'an contemplation. He is a core faculty member of the Kira Institute (www.kira.org), which explores the interface between modern, scientifically-framed perspectives and matters involving human values. He is currently collaborating with his Kira colleagues on books dealing with these subjects. Working on behalf of his teachers, Mr. Tainer has been the coauthor or editor of over eighteen books on Buddhism and Taoism (including *Dragon's Play*, and *Time, Space, Knowledge*). We had the pleasure of interviewing Steven while he was visiting at the Institute for Advanced Study in Princeton, New Jersey. One of the first things that Steven said when we told him we were writing a book on leadership was the following:

> "I am somewhat appalled by the notion that I have anything to say about being a leader, because I have spent so much of my life trying to avoid the leadership stereotype. It's a model that doesn't fit into what I am trying to do together with other people. There are many common teacher–student relationships that involve a "leader and led" logic. I try to avoid that. So much of what I say, I suspect, amounts to suggesting alternatives to many popular notions of leadership. I think many of the latter are regrettable. But if you're interviewing other people who don't agree, then of course nothing that I say should be taken to bear on their preference."

Not a promising start, you might think. But a lot of what Steven had to say was remarkably consistent with two other approaches to leadership, servant leadership and authentic leadership. An edited version of the full interview with Steven Tainer is contained in Chapter 9.

AUTHENTIC LEADERSHIP

The digital world has led many of us to lead compartmentalized lives. We have a self at home, another self at work, another one when we play, and multiple selves when we communicate on the Internet. We might even have an avatar with a distinct personality and value system. So the question becomes who is the real you? According to Gardner and colleagues, authentic leadership involves "both owning one's personal experiences (values, thoughts, emotions, and beliefs) and acting in accordance with one's true self (expressing what you really think and believe and behaving accordingly)."[16]

What does it mean to be authentic? Authenticity lies on a continuum. You can be more or less authentic but one of the ways that you can become more authentic is by increasing your self-awareness. This will then allow you to develop authentic relationships with your followers. Three related types of behaviors characterize authentic relationships:

1. Transparency, openness, and trust
2. Guidance toward worthy objectives
3. Emphasis on follower development

Authentic leaders also stress authentic followership and emphasize the development of the same types of authentic behavior so that followers can become authentic leaders themselves.

Authentic leadership proponents suggest that authentic leaders should produce several beneficial changes in followers. First, trusting relationships will be formed. Second, followers will be more engaged, enthusiastic, and committed to what they are doing. Third, followers will have a heightened sense of well-being. One other aspect of authentic leadership is particularly relevant to virtual work. Through the process of increasing self-awareness, authentic leaders better understand how to make sense of the world around them and also increase their ability to take perspective.

RETHINKING LEADERSHIP FOR THE VIRTUAL AGE

S.L. Washburn, the noted anthropologist wrote these words in his 1961 book, *Social Life of Early Man:*[17]

> Most of human evolution took place before the advent of agriculture when men lived in small groups, on a face-to-face basis. As a result human biology has evolved as an adaptive mechanism to conditions that have largely ceased to exist. Man evolved to feel strongly about few people, short distances, and relatively brief intervals of time; and these are still the dimensions of life that are important to him.

It is interesting to speculate what Washburn would make of the way that we interact today. Our interactions both at work and in life include some with people we have never met and probably never will meet. Yet we need to communicate and collaborate with them and with others that we may see rarely or every day. Early ideas about leadership were developed in a low-technology era and did not envision the issue of Virtual Distance that we describe in Chapter 1.

Based on the interviews with senior leaders in a variety of organizations in addition to the extensive research done to develop the Virtual Distance Model, it is clear that traditional approaches to leadership need to be rethought. It leads to the conclusion that leaders in the virtual age need different kinds of behaviors and new skills than those needed most by traditional leaders. The rest of this book details what those are and how to implement them.

NOTES

1. M. Bulmer, *Francis Galton: Pioneer of Heredity and Biometry*. (Baltimore, MD: Johns Hopkins University Press, 2003).
2. R.R. McCrae, and P.T. Costa, "Personality Trait Structure as a Human Universal," *American Psychologist*, (1997) 52, 509–516.
3. J.E. Bono, and T.A. Judge, "Personality and Transformational and Transactional Leadership: A Meta-Analysis," *Journal of Applied Psychology*, (2004) 89, 901–910.
4. Z. Aronson, R. Reilly, G. Lynn, "The Role of Leader Personality in New Product Development Success: An Examination of Teams Developing Radical and Incremental Innovations," *International Journal of Technology Management*, (2008) 44, 5–27.

5. R.J House, Path-Goal Theory of Leadership: Lessons, Legacy, and a Reformulated Theory. *Leadership Quarterly*, (1996) 7, 323–352.

6. K. Blanchard, S. Johnson, *The One Minute Manager* (New York: William Morrow, 1982)

7. W. Roberts, *Leadership Secrets of Attila the Hun* (New York: Warner Books, 1985)

8. Ibid., p. 63.

9. Ibid., p. 79.

10. K. Lowe, G. Kroeck, K. Sivasubramaniam. "Effectiveness Correlates of Transformational and Transactional Leadership: A Meta-Analytic Review of the MLQ Literature." *Leadership Quarterly*, (1996) 7, 385–425.

11. G. Sharp, *Gandhi Wields the Weapon of Moral Power: Salt March* (Greenleaf Books, 1983.

12. R. House, J. Howell, "Personality and Charismatic Leadership," *Leadership Quarterly*, (1992) 3, 81–108.

13. R.K. Greenleaf, *Servant Leadership: A Journey into the Nature of Legitimate Power and Greatness* (25th Anniversary Edition, Paulist Press, 2002), p. 21.

14. R. Nykiel, *Handbook of Marketing Research Methodologies for Hospitality and Tourism* (Binghamton, NY: Haworth Press, 2007), p. 259.

15. H. Kelleher, "A Culture of Commitment," *Leader to Leader* (1997) 4, 1–7.

16. W. Gardner, B. Avolio, F. Luthans, D. May, F. Walumbwa, "Can You See the Real Me? A Self-Based Model of Authentic Leader and Follower Development," *The Leadership Quarterly* (2005) 16, 342–372.

17. S.L. Washburn, *The Social Life of Early Man.* (1961)

CHAPTER **3**

Creating Context

A s you begin this chapter, take a look around. Where are you? What do you see? What do you hear? What do you smell? Perhaps you're sitting in a subway car where the lights flicker and the din of metal sliding along steel tracks is a constant reminder of your subterranean status. Or maybe you're sitting on a plane getting ready to take off, and relishing the time away from the non-stop flow of e-mail and cell phones jingle-jangling all day long.

In the former setting it's likely you're in a large city, getting bumped about as the train takes its turns, interrupting your concentration, and causing you to reread sentences to get the gist. In the latter situation it might be possible to read the entire book without a single jolt except for the occasional turbulence or a tap on the shoulder from the flight attendant asking you if you'd like something to drink. You might even have extra time to pause now and then, gaze out the window, and further consider an idea more carefully, maybe even jot down some notes to share later with colleagues.

No matter what your surroundings may be, though, the book is read within a physical context, which will impact both how you read it and what you remember from it. And together with this physical context, your point of view or "mental context," continuously contributes to how you judge what is written here. Meaning is derived, then, within this contextual framework that produces a "worldview"; a personal perspective, unique to every individual, shaped by all their experiences and life lessons, in much the same way as stream currents sculpt and smooth river rocks found at the shore.

Context is a critical element in understanding and interpreting information as well as individual behavior and it is an essential element in any workforce. Some organizational context is contained in mission statements and ephemeral corporate cultures. But in a more practical sense, context is the "stuff" of where people work, what they're thinking about day-to-day, and how they're reacting to, or provoking others. Context is the backdrop against which people decode communication, work together in teams, and build trust. Without it, Virtual Distance grows via value misalignment, misunderstandings in e-mails, and sometimes because one team member's circadian clock is simply out of whack with another's. In the virtual workforce, context, like that provided by traditional work environments, which we used to take for granted, becomes invisible. And leaders must color in the background so that the virtual workforce can see the picture they need to see in order to coalesce and collaborate in the connected age.

CONTEXT IN THE "OLD DAYS"

In traditional old-fashioned workplaces, where people walked through the same entrance every day and made their way to the office door with nameplate neatly affixed, where work was done from "9 to 5" and professionals lived in suburbs or cities familiar to all, context was easily recognized and shared. Others' worldviews unfolded seamlessly in hallway conversations, sporadic eruptions of political debate, and the haphazard discovery of joint interests.

Organizational context was transmitted through rigid, formal hier-archies in which controlled communication was sent from top to bot-tom in the form of memos, announcements, and unexpected "pop-ins" from the boss. Meetings were held in familiar, well-appointed confer-ence rooms, where authoritative positions were clearly visible by seat selection and respect doled out accordingly. Thus, the social order was reinforced, recognizable, and within conventional company context.

Additionally, personal information easily obtained about peers such as knowledge of a recent soccer win by a co-worker's son or daughter, or inside information about a boss's family difficulties could help an individual navigate the social undercurrents flowing in all directions throughout the shared workspace. This kind of intimacy provided more contextual perspective that helped inform and influence job behavior.

Besides context built by day-to-day routine and personal interaction, the larger organizational mission created broader connectivity when workers gathered together for presentations by senior managers or even the CEO, on a regular basis. During these meetings, past results and recent achievements would underscore common goals and provide a shared vision for the future. But what cemented this information into concrete context were informal discussions among participants that took place immediately afterwards, at the coffee machine or local diner. In so doing, group dynamics became bordered by a deeper organizational experience, a deeper context.

People, then, who lived and worked in the same general vicinity and who talked to each other face-to-face consistently formed relationships to construct well-built assumptions about the future, to determine one's place in it, and to strengthen their ability to adjust to changing circum-stances.

CONTEXT CHANGES IN THE DIGITAL AGE

But what of the new millennium workforce? Does it operate within a naturally occurring context coherently pulled together by familiar organizational structures and routine settings? With the rise of globally distributed teams, comprised of millions of people thrown together in fiber optic networks, likely never to meet, or who face each other only briefly, combined with an ever-increasing demand to meet productivity hurdles, the textured, gritty sights and sounds as well as social dynamics so clearly accessible in rituals past, have all but disappeared.

And while it is difficult, if not impossible, to recreate the context provided by a booming voice filling a large auditorium with inspiration, or assemble accurate representations of social status by people placed around a familiar table, establishing meaningful and extensive context is still critical. And building it, creating context, is one of the most important *new roles* for the leader in the digital age.

CONTEXTUAL LEADERSHIP AND THE VIRTUAL WORKFORCE

The virtual workforce tries to solve complex business problems and make sense of social situations with only a few disconnected snippets of project objectives and people profiles. But without the requisite context, soaring through cyberspace, albeit open, free and full of limitless connections, can also become confusing and sometimes frustrating for the virtual worker. To make more sense of the conundrum, consider the following passage:

> Aoccdrnig to rscheearch by the LngiusiitcDptanmeret at CmabrigdeUin- ervtisy, it deosn'tmttaer in wahtoredr the ltteers in a wrod are, the ol- nyiprmoetnttihng is taht the frist and lsatltteer be at the rghitpclae. The rset can be a total mses and you can sitllraed it wouthitporbelm. Tihs is bcuseae the huamnmniddeos not raederveylteter by istlef, but the wrod as a wlohe.[1]

At first blush the paragraph above seems a confusing concoction of nonsensical nomenclature. However, the reader quickly adapts and goes on to easily understand the mixed up letters. The mind can interpret jumbled jargon when it's anchored by proper placement of first and last letters with the rest floating randomly in between. When a reader can see the word as a whole, it is easily understood.

Today's leaders must, in essence, provide the first and last letters around otherwise encrypted information presented to the virtual workforce. They must make the fragmented virtual context whole. They must momentarily capture and package cyberspace chaos and continuously connect the dots for free floating far-flung teams.

Case One: Creating Global Context at Western Union

Susan Roser is the Senior Vice President of Global Service Support at Western Union, a worldwide money transfer company with over 300,000 agency locations spread all over the globe. Susan talks about the ways in which leadership has changed and the adjustments she's made in order to keep money moving freely to her customers.

"Leadership has definitely evolved. It used to be that you were the leader and your team was all around you; you were face to face all the time and you were cohabitated all the time. It is completely different for me now. I find that I spend more time in my office, which I never did before because my team isn't here for me to go walk out on the floor and chat with. But I'm on conference calls quite a bit of the day and on e-mail and on instant messaging. So I'm connected to my people.

But sometimes it strikes me as odd. You have to be a bit more creative and a little bit more trusting. You have to get to know your people and build that trust. And you've got to get to know their people and their centers [call centers] so that when you're talking to them, you've got that picture in your mind of their faces, their offices and generally what it looks like in the call center. You have to be able to answer the question, What's that noise in the background I'm hearing? and those kinds of things to appreciate their situations and recapture that one-on-one face time."

Susan puts people into context by keeping faces in mind and contextualizes distant workplaces by ably identifying low level swishing sounds or

(continued)

distant dings giving her crucial cues about a workforce thousands of miles away. But it's not just physical context that shores up clarity.

> It's also consistency of message. With this diverse group, I've had to really come up a couple of levels in terms of setting forth a vision because it has to encompass a myriad of functions and people. I set forth a vision statement and then break it down into no more than six objectives that we are driving to that apply to everybody. When we do our quarterly all-hands meeting, we all look at those objectives together.
>
> And actually, I'll take it a step further. From the corporate level, we have four strategy pillars. That's our mantra and that's everything we are working towards. I take my six objectives and align them to a pillar so that when we do our all-hands meetings we can show a clear picture as to how our objectives align to the corporate strategy.
>
> Then we look at what we have done so far to meet our objectives. So we are constantly reinforcing that same message. And my six objectives become the six objectives of my direct reports. Keeping that alignment all the way through the organization keeps us from drifting into silos or having people drift off on their own agendas or hobbies.

By painting a 360-degree view for her virtual workforce and their relation to organizational goals, using a mix of communication channels, both live and virtual, Susan generates coherent, shared mental models; she fuels **continuous cognitive context**.

While Susan's consistent messages and regular meetings provide much-needed reference reinforcements, effective leadership would not be possible without her concomitant travel activities to make customary contact to build meaningful relationships.

> I am personally making quarterly visits to each of the sites. And during those visits, I spend time with my direct reports. I do round-tables with employees. I take large groups out to lunch and celebrate whatever they want.
>
> I hold skip levels with all my directs' directs. I go down a level and have one-on-ones with all of them. I ask them what challenges they are facing, how is their career going, what are they focused on,

and how can I help them. And so really, I feel more like family when I go to those [call] centers.

The first time I went to each of the centers they made a big deal about everything. They treated me like royalty, which was great. But now it's gotten to be like I'm just one of the team. And that's where I want it to be. That has been very effective in really keeping me connected to people.

Like many of the other executives interviewed, Susan describes global travel as needed to build context for both herself, as well as for the rest of her organization. But that's the easy part. The real question is:

How do you keep that love alive after the meeting is over?

Within the virtual workforce, teams shift and change like sand dunes in the desert; forming, dissipating, and re-emerging in different arrangements. Workers belong to many social networks that sometimes coalesce, or collide, or float about in the virtual abyss. Reorganizations abound with dizzying speed, making it difficult for any given person to stay mentally tethered to one group versus another, one organization versus another, or even one time period versus another.

It's easy, then, for a worker to feel disconnected from a central purpose or company mission in this environment. They need leaders like Susan to grab onto in digital space to reassure and refocus them.

CONSTANCY AND LEADERSHIP: A TIE THAT BINDS

Some projects are long-term and have a strategic focus that requires people to think into the future and imagine new products and services. Other deliverables are often said to be "due yesterday" because they are utterly urgent. One minute a virtual foot-soldier might be working on the former and is then pulled over to do something for the latter. The phone rings in the middle of the night and it's a question from a person in an office on the other side of the globe. As sleep is shaken off clarity must develop quickly to solve a customer's problem.

In the global workforce, a person can literally be in two or three or even ten or twelve time-zones at the same time when huddled around a conference phone or donning a digital headset along with other distant team members calling in from around the world. Combined with constant interruptions from e-mail, instant messages, cell phone calls, and more, this chronological cognitive jostling further fractures attention and adds to information overload and excessive multitasking that's costing $650 billion in lost productivity per year in the United States alone.[2]

But to think that any of this is likely to change soon or that we are somehow only temporarily afflicted with attention deficit disorder would be unrealistic. However, establishing a constant, something familiar that can be relied upon, no matter the moment, can provide much needed grounding and tighter, tangible ties to unforeseen pieces of what can be an invisible maze of unrelenting tasks and turned-around times. *That constant, in many cases, is a good leader.*

Case Two: Constancy in Motion at Merck

Robert McMahon is the President of U.S. Commercial Operations at Merck & Co., Inc. He is responsible for over 4,000 sales representatives as well as numerous functional units. We began each interview with a general question about the nature and scope of the executive's responsibilities. Here's what Bob had to say.

"I came to Merck from Arthur Andersen where I was an auditor in the late 1970s. I joined Merck's finance group in internal audit and worked through finance for several years and eventually found my way into field sales in the mid 1980s. I have worked in various sales, marketing, or hybrid jobs including economic affairs and joint ventures for my whole career.

In the late 1990s I assumed leadership for a large sales organization here in the U.S. as vice president. I ran the joint venture with Schering Plough for four years from its inception through 2004. I managed the Arthritis and Analgesia business, and starting about four years ago, I began leading a business unit in the U.S. and most recently the entire U.S. Pharma business.

I guess I have a general management background. I've been for-tunate to kind of grow up in the Merck organization and have been given a lot of opportunities to lead larger and larger pieces of the business which have allowed me to do a variety of things including launching four or five products and managing through some inter-esting relationships with Johnson & Johnson and Schering Plough. And now, in effect, to lead Merck into a new era in terms of how we interface with our customers.

So I'm pretty homogeneous in my pedigree in terms of who I've worked for. But if you look at my resume you'll find lots of zigs and zags in terms of the kinds of things that I've been doing."

The first thing you notice is that Bob has been with Merck for over 20 years. As time passes, this kind of tenure may become rare. But what's important is the breadth of experience Bob has with many different kinds of initiatives, one building upon the next, bringing increasing responsibilities with each "zig" and "zag."

Via a combination of longevity as well as latitudinal experience, Bob brings a stable and informed perspective to his followership. Using the com-plementary contextual dimensions of consistent communications around vision clarity and future direction, Bob can be considered a **contextual constant**.

We asked him how he is able to set such a high standard among such a dispersed set of resources.

"I think you've got to start from a strong foundation. First of all I think people need to have a sense of who you are. I think you have to be a credible, a thoughtful, and a substantial leader to make different choices about how to get in front of your people. When I say in front of them, I mean through a wide mix of different approaches. I've invested a lot of time over the years getting people to believe in me—doing the kinds of things that convince people that I'm a trusted, valuable leader they will want to follow.

And I've done that mostly by virtue of my actions, but also by how I've spoken to people, whether it's face-to-face or in any number of other ways. So, at the end of the day, I think you're enabled by how well you establish yourself in the organization and that gives you the luxury to communicate in a variety of ways."

(continued)

Developing virtual workforce leader qualities involves honing perceived constancy by becoming aware of the many dynamic forces that propel people forward. Bob describes one of the many challenges:

"A major hurdle was frankly getting comfortable with who I was talking to. So, I was a representative in the mid 1980s, and by the time I was leading representatives in a meaningful way, it was the early 1990s. The change in that population and how they wanted to be spoken to, how they wanted to listen, what they were willing to receive and how the information needed to be framed was significantly different than when I was a representative. And, I was a fairly old representative even when I was a representative. Now that I have 4,000 representatives out there who are at the age of my children and, in many cases, younger than my children, I've really had to work very hard to understand what it is that they need to hear and how they need to hear it."

Bob demonstrates meta-cognition or "outside-in" thinking; an ability to see beyond ones' self, to become aware of others and their needs, to internalize many sets of unique circumstances, identities and personalities, and to incorporate those into the transference of global goals to a broad base of technologically tethered workforces. It requires a leader to share *comprehensive context*.

But leaders like Bob cannot do this alone.

"The first thing you have to have, Karen, and I've made mistakes here, is you have to have people well-positioned in the organization to tell you the truth. Blatant, hard, sometimes difficult truth about how good you are with respect to actually getting through to people. And, they have to be positioned at all levels and in all aspects of the organization such that you're getting it real-time and you're getting it when you need it. I've learned from that."

The leader as the *contextual constant* has many critical responsibilities, not the least of which is to stay relevant to a population poised on the precipice of uncertainty. Bob uses his well-established and trusted presence as a force that brings confidence to the thousands of people who depend on him and whose work revolves around trying to bring better health to the population. Bob also leverages a deep well of experience, including both successes as well as some missteps, and passes the lessons learned on to others.

STORYTELLING AND LEADERSHIP: A CRUCIAL PAIR

With formal hierarchies disintegrating, a leader has to be able to tell his or her story in a way that remains engaging and motivating to unseen, often text-based audiences. In the "old days" when the leader could share his or her presence, and not just the message, in a large room standing on top a platform podium, with a big metal microphone attached to a lit shelf, formal status combined with language and word use, intonation, and gaze could jettison anxious listeners out of their seats and into action. But that strategy alone, used for leading a virtual workforce, is almost completely bankrupt.

Leaders now need to weave together bits of information about themselves, others, and organizational goals to form fiery stories in text and pictures for audiences that can vary by as many as four generations, are culturally diverse, and are strewn throughout landmasses sprinkled around the globe.

Case Three: Crayola, Context, and the Craft of Storytelling

Cheri Sterman is the Director of Child Development and Consumer Relationships at Crayola. She is directly responsible for one of the world's most recognized brands. At the same time she is also charged with creating new products and services to meet the many changing needs of families around the world. Cheri believes that storytelling is a key ingredient to good leadership in the digital age and that it's not just for kids anymore.

"In our Consumer Affairs department we just recently celebrated several of our employees who have now entered the

(continued)

100,000 Contact Club. Those individuals have spoken to 100,000 consumers and we have several people in that club. We have people who have been with us, talking with consumers everyday for more than a decade. In a field that might have an average tenure of 12 months, our average tenure is over 12 years.

There's a couple of reasons for this. The first is people here feel incredibly fortunate to be able to work on the Crayola brand. The brand looms bigger than what we make. People have such a connection with it. So that's part of it.

I also think it has to do with how excited our employees are about being here. One of the things I ask my staff members and people in workshops I lead is "What's your story about; why are you here?" There are a couple of different stories people tell. And they don't realize people are telling stories all day, every day. Right? We all do; going to a meeting, we chat with people; we get on the phone, we chat with people. It's just human interaction. And so part of the story we tell people is "Who I Am." And then part of the story we tell people is "Why I'm Here." And I'm here because I am so passionate about creativity and I think that becomes really contagious. It's really something that my staff is able to connect with. I'm sure this love of what we do at Caryola affects the Consumer Affairs staff tenure."

Cheri cherishes the fact that she works for Crayola and impacts so many people's lives in a positive way. As a leader, her motivation is fueled by a dual love for creativity and children; ideally suited for Crayola. It is in this context, it is for this *reason*, that she has built enormous social capital among her staff, customers, and other key stakeholders.

Cheri transmits her zeal for constant creation and re-creation of the human spirit through storytelling; about herself as well as the lives of the families that have been transformed by the products she represents. By doing so, Cheri builds *contagious context*.

Referring to Larry Prusak's book, *Storytelling in Organizations*, Cheri continues.

"All animals do a welcoming ritual. Think about what happens when you go into a meeting and you see people. You're gathering in an office, you're gathering in a conference setting. There is this exchange of stories. People start talking about how they got there or what their trip was like or their family or whatever. They start exchanging stories.

And it's not that what is said really matters. Nobody probably even remembers the details of it. We're socially wired to do this. To tell stories. It's the way we greet others that helps us feel comfortable with the people around us—before we settle down to talk business. And I love the comment that he [Larry Prusak] makes. He says, all animals do it, dogs sniff each other, humans tell stories. It's our welcoming ritual.

Okay. So if you're in a virtual workplace, how do you do that welcoming ritual? What can you do in a virtual setting that allows this exchange? It's not what you're saying. I mean how many virtual meetings start right off with some kind of agenda? Right?"

Cheri understands the power of storytelling—how useful it can be but also how stories can set the stage for misconceptions that last.

"A story is a shared experience. And the purpose of the story is to make the impersonal personal. So maybe another way that we look in the crystal ball if we're all going to have to be doing more of this virtually and over distance, is how do we dial up the storytelling part of our virtual interactions to make them more personal? If you define a story as a shared experience then you have to think about what's the purpose of the story.

It's not like you have to learn this whole new skill set. You actually are a storyteller. The challenge is: to be a good storyteller you have to stop being a bad one.

And then you have to start monitoring the stories you tell. When you listen to someone, are they pining away for retirement? Are they frustrated, are they victims? Or, is every story that comes out of their mouth positive. When I teach, I ask participants to consider four types of stories; Who I Am, Why I'm Here, What I Can Teach You, and Where I Want the Outcome to Go. For the first, I ask them to make a list of what they want other people to think of them.

Nobody puts on their list that they want to be thought of as the victim, or pity me, or that I'm a frustrated one. And yet very few

(continued)

people monitor their stories—especially in e-mail and other kinds of virtual communications. Okay. So start editing them so that they are what you want people to know about you."

Cheri's customer service representatives add to the Crayola story all day, every day. They are the customer-facing leaders of the company. So what story do they tell? What context do they provide their consumers?

"We tell our staff that their job is to be the voice of the trusted friend, that Crayola's brand voice is the trusted friend. When they are on that phone and when they answer it, that's what they are. They are that person's trusted friend. We will come through for you. We will uphold the promise and meet your expectations."

And how does Cheri's leadership style, designed around creating context through engaging storytelling, result in returns to the company? You will find the answer in one of Crayola's thousands of customer stories. It's called, "My Family Celebrates the Crayola Promise."

"My husband and I were busy barbecuing with last-minute preparations for an extended family birthday celebration for our three-year-old. We left our two sons sitting on our king size bed to watch TV so we could cook. I had just used your washable markers to draw a large posterboard sign. Our three and five year-olds quickly got busy doing their own party preparations. They opened the craft box that I admittedly left carelessly sitting on the bed and dove into the box of Crayola washable markers. Shortly after a blood-curdling scream interrupted the festivities. My husband rushed toward the bedroom to find me uncontrollable. I had found that my sons had tattooed themselves from head to toe with multi-colored scribbles. The youngest was chewing on the writing end of a bright blue marker. His face, clothing, arms, legs looked as if he had just been to a baby tattoo parlor.

Further investigation revealed that he had written with marker all over our bed sheets, our comforter, and the antique, handmade quilt that my deceased grandmother made for me as a child. On the sheets where he hadn't actually written, he had obviously become fascinated with how the marker, if held in one spot, would form a large pool of color. There were several large pools of blue spots all over the linens. I had barely enough time to wash off the boys before the guests arrived.

Well, Crayola, it is the next day now and the entire incident is a memory. That's right, I just said a memory. Despite chewing on your non-toxic product, my son is fine, but the miracle is that the linens washed perfectly. No trace of anything. Thank you for living up to your word. When you call markers washable, you keep your promise."

Crayola customers are closely wed to the promise of the brand and Cheri is the highly charged evangelist who ensures they never want a divorce. And she takes the responsibility of having a big bully pulpit, both "live" and virtual, seriously.

"Leaders are telling stories all day, every day. To be the best one has to constantly be asking, 'Is that the story I want to tell?'"

Who among us doesn't remember holding a uniquely named crayon between our little fingers? Some say what they remember most is the smell; others say the taste. But no matter what the sensational recall, it's clear that Crayola contributes to millions and millions' of childhood experiences, becoming part of our life context. And Cheri personifies a leadership style well suited for the charge.

CONCLUSION

The virtual workforce is comprised of people whose communications are diffused through the Internet and who all use varying frames from which to interpret and assign meaning to others' actions and words. In most situations, little in the way of context is now known in the same way it organically presented itself in firm structural formations or shared physical spaces of the past. Weaving together a whole picture about one's colleagues and mission at any given time, or determining the proper perspective from which to interpret discourse from an e-mail or other electrified communication is no longer a completely natural process.

Therefore, leaders in this new era have to be strong sense-makers; bringing context to virtual teams that need to operate in the right frame, a common frame, that is difficult to see from any singular, sometimes isolated perch. What the leader of today has to do differently, as compared to times gone by, is to create context in a variety of ways for a set of people that may never physically share more than the same bandwidth and whose worldviews may be invisible to teammates who have a "need to know."

NOTES

1. Illinoisloop.org. *Phonics is a Fraud?* www.illinoisloop.org/phonicsfraud.html
2. See Steve Lohr, "Is Information Overload a $650 Billion Drag on the Economy?" *New York Times*, December 20, 2007, http://bits.blogs.nytimes.com/2007/12/20/is-information-overload-a-650-billion-drag-on-the-economy/

CHAPTER 4

Cultivating Communities

The notion of community building in business has been around for a long time. In the 1950s and 1960s, many corporations expected employees to participate in local communities in part because of the aftermath of World War II and in part because leadership at the time was espousing the virtues of volunteering. "Ask not what your country can do for you but what you can do for your country," said President John F. Kennedy in his inaugural speech.

Donating discretionary time to neighborhood charities, participating in local clubs like the Elks, the Moose Lodge, and so on, or coaching youth baseball helped buoy professional careers. In fact, performance was judged less than stellar if community building was absent from personal activities. It was part of a social contract; employees worked to advance inside the corporate kingdom while making time to "do good" for society outside company enclaves.

Recall from Chapter 1 that in the 1950s a majority of Americans thought that corporations were good for the country. Most people trusted executives. Whether community building had a direct correlation is unknown; however, it would make sense that high visibility and positive contributions within local communities would boost overall perception of corporate leadership in a local culture and beyond.

But community building has taken on a whole new meaning since the Internet pervaded our global town in the late 1990s and early 2000s. Even at the beginning of the dotcom boom websites were relatively easy to build. So entrepreneurs as well as grassroots organizers began calling anything that drew people to a particular website, especially around specific interests such as skydiving, gender equality, golf, and so on, a community. And the companies behind the ether-engine were called community builders. This led to some skepticism because the word community was over-used, over-hyped, and over-run. In other cases, as demonstrated by the multiple phenomena of Facebook, MySpace, Twitter, Spaces and other social networks, the notion of community was easier to see. However, despite these viral community success stories, business organizations are still struggling to mimic their achievements and activate advancement of global, corporate agendas.

But among leaders who have stellar track records shaping successful virtual workforce strategies, we've found that the building and cultivating of broad communities is an integral factor in sustained growth.

Case One: Community Development at Alcatel-Lucent

Guido Petit is the Director of the Alcatel-Lucent Technical Academy or ALTA—a program designed to recognize individuals who have made exceptional contributions to the technological and innovative leadership of the company. His home base is Antwerp, Belgium but Guido travels the world developing the ALTA community. ALTA is comprised of the top 500 in the company gaining membership through nomination. Membership is limited to three years which means that each year there are, on average, 170 open positions for new or renewed members.

"We are using this community of 500 members as a kind of think tank to come up with proposals on how we can improve the R&D effectiveness in the company. And this is across the boundaries of the organization. These members provide the main set of innovation, networking, knowledge sharing and best practices sharing. They are organized according to chapter. For instance, you have IT chapters everywhere in the world, but also in the Academy, we have a chapter in Belgium, a chapter in France, in the United States, in Canada, in India, and in China. So in every place where we have a critical mass of Academy members, we create a chapter that is chaired by co-chairs and a local chairperson who takes the initiative together with others in what we call all-time members of the Alcatel-Lucent Technical Academy to come up with proposals that are in line with the mission of the academy.

It is a distributed organization where I have delegated responsibilities to the different chapters, co-chairpersons, and chairpersons. So they have the freedom to initiate a number of activities that are in line with the mission of the Academy that have to be qualified for instance as local stakeholders and they also get the permission to fund some of the initiatives. So for instance we set up events regularly in the various chapters, for networking and knowledge sharing purposes where we invite internal as well as external distinguished guest speakers to give a talk of interest. And this talk of interest is open to anybody in the company. It is recorded so that people can view it later if they were not able to attend it physically in one location or when other people in other companies are interested in the topics, but of course, can't be present in Belgium.

Let's say we talk about best practices especially. We invite guest speakers from different companies not related to our business; chemical companies, the pharmaceutical sector companies, automobile sector companies like Mercedes Benz, to give a talk of their innovation best practices.

And when we see some best practices that can also be applied inside our company, we [ALTA] become the network of experts. We promote these best practices inside our company. So that's to give you an example of how we share best practices that we see

(continued)

internally or that we see also externally. And then best practices with regard to innovation, because, yes, every company today can't survive if it doesn't come up with new products that generate new revenue for the company."

By developing communities where members are expected to *act* on behalf of the rest, such as in the case of sharing best practices for example, Guido develops more than a community; he builds *co-operative communities*—groups in which people don't simply gather information and learn from one another, but are comprised of self-motivated individuals who carry out action on behalf of the group for the betterment of the entire organization.

And it is all done on a voluntary basis—a condition common to every organization that relies upon employees' discretionary time for community development. And this can sometimes pose a challenge. Guido continues:

"Well, there are different challenges. First of all, all the people who become members of the Academy, they are volunteers to do some duties on top of daily business. And so, if we say they are going to act as a factory thinker to help organize functions in the organization or to act as a think tank to come up with proposals to improve the R&D effectiveness, because all activities are on top of daily duties and obviously these people cannot spend ten percent of their working time to achieve the mission of the academy.

Which means that if some people have concrete ideas on how to let's say work out a proposal that generates some obvious value for their department or for their division or for the company as a whole, they have to do that together with other people who believe in the proposition. And these other people, they can be located in other locations or in other countries. And then it's up to them to connect, to find these people who have the same energy and belief in the proposition and who would like to work together virtually to work out the proposal and to come with an action plan that can be implemented.

And of course people don't have the possibility to see each other on a daily basis or to have face-to-face meetings typically. So this means that everything has to be done by mail, by phone, by conference call and so on and so on. But of course, are still admitted by the chapter chairs and co-chairs in the different countries.

Now, this is only possible when you have committed and multi-faceted people. You have people in the Academy who are only interested in the recognition and the title but who have no interest in all the activities and initiatives we plan. But there are all sorts of other people who joined the Academy because they share the same views and values of the Academy and the importance of network-ing, knowledge sharing, best practices sharing, and innovation. It's exactly by counting on these positively oriented people that things can be realized in the Academy.

So I don't put any energy in people who I would say have a neg-ative attitude. I only work with the positive people in the company and put all my energy in those people, because I know that energy is well-spent and these people are also going to feel that energy. It's on both sides and then some things will happen. And of course, the negative people, they will follow later on when they see that some added value has been generated by the positive people. So that any importance, I would say, that people management prac-tice, that you focus first on the positive people to realize something and then once you have realized something, you give feasibility to it worldwide and then probably the more skeptical people, they are going to follow later on when they see that there is a positive outcome."

A community of positive-minded people is a cornerstone of any strong community like that of ALTA; it is a *constructive community* whose members embody activist energy and fuel further developments by finding ways to increase proposal potential.

As Guido's success with ALTA shows, community can be a powerful force within company configurations comprised of the virtual workforce.

But long before the virtual workforce became a permanent fixture in corporations, the concept of community building in business had taken shape. One of the most eloquent supporters was a man by the name James A. Autry, President of the Meredith Corporation's magazine group until his retirement in 1991 and a renowned poet from the delta region of

Mississippi and Tennessee. In an interview with Bill Moyers in his book, *The Language of Life: A Festival of Poets*,[1] he revealed intriguing insights about his belief in community; thoughts very much outside the norm as compared to most industrial and post-industrial efficiency-based perspectives of the time.

Bill Moyers: Do you experience in the business world any of the love and community so palpable in your experience in Mississippi?

Autry: Yes, I do.

Moyers: But we don't think of the business world that way.

Autry: I know we don't, but to me an important part of the business world is trying to get through the macho veneer we've built around business and get to the feelings, which are at the heart of business. I keep saying business is life, life is business, so where did we get this macho, tough guy stuff? In fact, you spend 60 percent of your waking hours on the job—you celebrate, you suffer, you worry, you feel anxiety and pain and fear and jealousy and joy right there in the workplace every day—and that is what I try to get into poetry. In a way, what I'm saying is if we deal with the humanity of business, then the business will take care of itself.

Moyers: All those metaphors of competition that spill over from sports to business.

Autry: Exactly. Sports and even battle metaphors are often used in business. I hardly use the word "team" in business; I use "community" much more frequently. If I'm involved in anything that is of great moment in business, it is trying to help evolve or discover a new vocabulary for people in business to use with one another.[2]

Autry, then, offers a different take on business reality—a more human-based view. And he surmises that starting with the concerns of the human community is the best way to understand that business itself is a human endeavor. Therefore, it's only appropriate that we turn next to one of the oldest tech companies on the planet to see how collaboration technology has evolved and serves not only as a core product offering, but also as a way to keep a community of over 300,000 people tied together closely.

During the early part of the new millennium, it was widely reported that IBM used the power of collaboration to transform the way it held meetings.[3] Instead of one-way communications, massive meetings were established where thousands of employees gathered online to share views in real time using tools such as polling and online voting. Individuals from the most remote corners of the world began to influence the course of things to come. IBM did not stop there. They built an entire division around Social Software to promote its benefits and build advancements. And it is paying off.

Case Two: Input By Masses: How Leadership and Social Software Transformed IBM

Gina Poole is the Vice President of Software Group Marketing 2.0 at IBM. Starting out with zero direct reports from her home base in Raleigh's Research Technology Park, Gina has built a massive delegation of social software ambassadors and collaboration gurus. We asked Gina how she created critical mass using community volunteers.

"We tap into volunteers all over IBM who want to share their knowledge of social software. Today we have around 650 people from 35 countries who educate their peers, run enablement sessions, and evangelize tools and skills to help their colleagues become more productive using social software. These evangelists, who we call BlueIQ Ambassadors, don't work directly for me, and many are not even in the software division—they come from our hardware business, our sales teams, our services business. They're motivated by the opportunity to share their expertise in a certain area of social software, and by the chance to build their own skills. They also like being actively involved in a virtual community of people who share their passion.

(continued)

As a result, more people influence my mission to leverage the tools in our social software portfolio, including tools coming from IBM Research, to help our internal teams be more effective. More people can find and connect with experts and find and share the information they need—thereby creating a stronger culture of sharing in IBM."

Like Guido's ALTA group, IBM's BlueIQ Ambassadors consist of people who do not have to commit any time at all. However, those who do engage in shaping the thoughts and futures of many across a wide spectrum of IBM's massive workforce.

"We don't require specific time commitments from these Ambassadors, and we leave the type of contribution open to their level of interest and ability. They can spend an hour a week, ten hours a week—whatever they have time to do. Some Ambassadors offer one-on-one clinic hours that help people get started using a social software technology. For example, how do I start a blog? What's blogging etiquette, etc? Others do what we call lunch and learn education sessions, and often these are virtual sessions. And some of them do what we call jump-start consulting, where they'll do an internal consulting engagement with a specific team to understand the team's pain points, goals, and objectives. They'll help the team select the right social software tools for their needs and help enable the team on the tools and processes."

By keeping the BlueIQ ambassador community focused on key activities, Gina creates *confluent communities*—groups of people who set similar expectations for thousands across the worldwide organization. But it's not just confluence that is required to keep others outside the ambassador community engaged. In fact, Gina knows that while bottom-up initiatives are key to corporate community building, unlike more free-wheeling, non-corporate networks like those mentioned earlier, so too, is top-down buy-in.

"We do a lot of internal communications to share success stories, advocate the Ambassador program, and make individuals, teams, managers, and executives aware that we can help them. People involved with BlueIQ always mention the Ambassador program, and encourage others to join. We award our most active volunteers with a Most Valuable Ambassador award, and highlight the awards on our intranet and through other communications. This bottoms-up momentum is probably the most powerful way to drive social software adoption. But I think there's also an important top-down component to it as well. The executives and managers have to view social software adoption as valuable, encourage it, and in most cases, do it themselves."

Gina possesses long-term *community commitment*. As a matter of fact, it was community building that led her into the executive suite at IBM.

"At one time I led strategy and operations across one of the software divisions. While in that job, I ran into someone who had worked for me previously, on running a small IBM website about Java. We got to talking about a gap that IBM had in reaching the 10 million developers in the world—that we really didn't have the mindshare with them, that they weren't always aware of what IBM had to offer, and that they didn't necessarily have the kind of skills in open standards, which was becoming our strategic direction. So we talked about the need to do more to engage and influence that community. Together we started a little skunk works project to create a web community for the developer audience, as well as an end-to-end marketing program that would achieve better awareness and be engaged with the community. We grew that little start-up from nothing into a pretty decent sized worldwide organization that's been very successful for IBM. It grew to six million members and generates about $300 million a year in lead revenue. It was exciting to do a start up within a big company."

From zero to $300 million in revenue—Gina's success with the online developer community is more than impressive. And Gina knows that she must recognize and reward her ambassadors if they are to make the same kind of impact. In describing the most important elements in keeping people engaged, Gina points to ongoing feedback and acknowledgment for jobs well done.

"It is important to give constructive feedback, but also to be sure to give positive feedback and celebrate things. On a team call this

(continued)

> morning, I shared successes from my organization and gave out some awards. One of my employees is on the cover of a marketing magazine, selected as Digital Marketer of the Year, so I made a visual to share with everyone in the meeting. People will follow someone who they see as having a good vision, who is excited about the job, and who will take care of them. You don't have to yell at people or micromanage them. If you've created the environment and the vision and the support structure, they'll work like crazy and you can't stop them."

Gina Poole has constructed a vibrant productive community within the confines of a corporate crawl space. She has changed the way IBM does business with their developers and in so doing, created highly profitable revenue streams. She also secured a steady stream of collaboration experts to help with community development among huge swaths of IBMers.

Leaders like Gina and Guido know that to successfully build critical mass among people who are worlds apart geographically, culturally, and even spiritually, engendering healthy communities is key. They inspire people to act on behalf of a group, resulting in long-term, organic well-being that benefits both the individual and the company.

But this also requires top-down leadership for virtual communities to flourish in the context of other organizational matters. For Guido, a major imperative is to get local chairs of ALTA involved, for without local support global efforts would be stifled. Gina notes that management support for ambassadors helps them to pursue social software interests—no matter their function or formal tether.

CONCLUSION

For leaders that make the virtual workforce whiz, cultivating community leads to other big pay-offs like reducing Virtual Distance which in turn leads to increased innovation, higher job satisfaction, and better leader effectiveness. While physical distance is an issue in each and every scenario described, it becomes less of an impediment when people are working toward common goals and feel they are interdependent on one another for success—as is the case in ALTA and BlueIQ Ambassadors. This kind of attachment is what builds strong relationships and reduces affinity distance. By decreasing this most toxic element of Virtual Distance, communications easily flow, people understand the meaning that others actually intend, and no matter what the dispersion pattern of resources, the occasional voice in the dark or words on a screen help to keep people bound together moving toward a felt sense of shared future and fate. Therefore, operational distance also wanes and the overall Virtual Distance profile for community members; between themselves and those they serve, is relatively small. And with decreasing Virtual Distance comes increased trust, and those who trust each other tend to draw people in who are also open to trusting.[4] And a positive, building process gets even more momentum and the community grows.

Community development is nothing new but the way in which communities grow in the context of corporate containers in the Internet age is completely different than the way community development first came on the scene. But any attempt to define it seems to run counter to what many believe is at its heart—engagement, experience, action, and self-sacrifice; all very tacit in nature and not easily accessible through words. Also since anything resembling massive hits to a website is called a community, and in some cases describes or defines that community, those trying to grasp their power for corporate gain tend to shun the very idea. But as we have seen, great leaders who create co-operative and constructive communities, fostering community commitment across boundaries are making many innovative products and finding ways to leverage collaboration in the discovery of new science. They are believers in community development as a potent path on which to gain insight and drive revenue. However, as we will see in Chapter 5, lone leaders do not do this alone.

NOTES

1. B. Moyers, *The Language of Life: A Festival of Poets* (New York: Broadway Books, 1995).
2. Ibid., pp. 22–23.

3. *BusinessWeek* (August 7, 2006). "Big Blue Brainstorm: IBM is Putting Some 100,000 Heads Together for an Online Innovation Jam." www.businessweek. com(magazine(content(06_32(b3996062.htm?chan(technology_ceo+guide+to+ technology Reference to news article about JAM sessions.

4. K. Sobel Lojeski, R. Reilly, *Uniting the Virtual Workforce: Transforming Leadership and Innovation in the Globally Integrated Enterprise* (Hoboken, NJ: John Wiley & Sons, 2008) Chapter 3.

CHAPTER 5

Co-Activating New Leaders

When looking at the hundreds of pages of interviews collected for this book, comprised of comments from leaders across a wide spectrum of industries, it soon became clear they had many things in common and that a new kind of leader was emerging; those that seek out others in the virtual workforce with leader potential and enable them to operate freely and establish their own leadership credentials.

As already described, each leader finds a way to create context where it is often lost in virtual workforces. They also cultivate viral communities. In addition, each leader recognizes and internalizes a simple reality. Their leadership alone is not enough when it comes to large, networked organizations consisting of people that sit within the bounds of traditional organizational structures but who are also part of the new virtual workforce. These leaders know that to succeed they may need to draw on people who work for other organizations, or for themselves, or simply gravitate toward the organization's orbit from time to time. These kinds of organizations are what Sam Palmisano of IBM calls "globally integrated enterprises."[1] In such dense and relatively disorganized business models, corporate goals and ambitious strategic outcomes are not possible without building multiple leadership arenas throughout the organization.

Unlike models that espouse the leader as the singular transformative figure, today's leaders co-opt others to make things happen—putting themselves aside at times (servant leadership), asserting their authority at other times (transactional leadership), but recruiting others to lead at *all* times. This quality is different than shared leadership or distributed leadership. It's not shared because the leader does not somehow break down his/her responsibilities and dole out some and keep others. It's not simply distributed because that would imply that it's just a matter of physicality and as we know from the Virtual Distance Model, physicality is not the most difficult challenge. Instead we are talking about *co-activating new leaders.*

Co-activating leaders expend enormous energy to maintain momentum among many different yet coordinated leader efforts within the confines of informal social networks as well as formal organizational structures. And unlike pure influence models that have come before it, co-activating new leaders, while remaining central figures in establishing large-scale vision and mission, often play a very small if not infinitesimal role in leading the virtual workforce directly. However, control is not part of this equation. Instead what's required is a high comfort level with ambiguity and uncertainty, not just with market conditions, or one's own career path, but with the state of the virtual workforce as well.

Old leadership models also include the idea of delegation—but that's different as well. Delegation implies a direct link that pulls the follower back to the leader. If a leader delegates a certain task to a follower, then that follower is responsible to the leader and ultimately, is assessed on her/his performance on that task. While delegation is still an important part of good management practice, it does not capture the essence of distinctly unique leader challenges in the Digital Age. For that, a whole new paradigm is needed.

Case One: HP Harnesses New Leader Models

Phil McKinney is the Vice President and Chief Technology Officer of Hewlett-Packard's Personal Systems group. He's responsible for all products HP sells at large electronic retailers except for printers. In addition, Phil is the head of HP's Innovation Program Office as well as Industry Standards and Ergonomics. His leadership reach is vast.

> "The challenge I have is I have 310,000 employees. How do I go find the absolute best and brightest employee, no matter where they live, and get them plugged into a team to build absolutely killer products?"

Phil knows that with 310,000 employees, located around the world, there is no way he can do the leadership job alone. He uses several leadership practices to co-activate others. One involves enabling social networking and creating the conditions for enough face time so that when virtual workforce members need to solve difficult problems, they can reach out and contact someone in their collegial circle.

We asked him how he manages the challenges of a globally distributed workforce that has to figure out, largely on their own, how to develop a social network and become part of the corporate community, when the natural state is to have more screen time than face time.

> "That's kind of a tough one to answer. When I'm evaluating poten-tial leaders or I'm looking at leaders that I think have been highly successful in their careers, its leaders who have, at least from within HP, who have done rotations, who have stayed in the field, who've crossed multiple geographies. It isn't somebody who's spent their entire career simply based in the United States sitting in corporate headquarters and climbing the ladder in the traditional sense. In fact, at HP, one of the criteria that's used to identify potentially what we call high performing executives for promotion are those that have had at least one if not two or three rotations into different regions and not always back to the same regions. So you know, spend a year or two in Japan, spend a year or two in France and then you're back to the United States. It's something as diverse as that.

(continued)

It's also about building up a social network. In HP as in any large organization, you've got the formal way of getting things done and you've got the informal way of getting things done. And the informal way is extremely more efficient. And the way to get the informal things done is through the process of having that social network. Having worked with enough people across different organizations such that if you need to get something done, you've built up social capital with somebody else in the organization. Whether it be something as simple as procurement to help get a PO through the process to something as tough as you're running into a product challenge and you know somebody who's on a rotation in a different part of the world on a different job, but you know that person knows the information you need and the ability to reach out and get to them. And have them get engaged and volunteer their time to help solve your problem.

And the key in building that social network is in the ability to understand how you build your own internal social network in such a way that you know how to put your hands on people that can help you and help the organization be successful. And historically, that's all been fairly hard to do from the standpoint of just face time and just finding those people. Inside of HP we work pretty hard to try to help find those people with common interests, common backgrounds or even different backgrounds to find each other to participate and create sub social networks inside of HP."

Phil knows that for people to get promoted and to enliven their careers within HP, social networking is key. Phil co-activates others by placing a lot of value on gaining real-life cross-cultural experience and in this manner Phil is a *global experience advocate*—a key characteristic of co-activating leaders.

And it's not just employees that Phil co-activates through his leadership. In fact, to build the best products in the world, Phil believes that it's best to engage the local community in that effort as well.

"We sell products into maybe 180 countries so you obviously have the cultural challenges of understanding. For us it's about knowledgeable employees and understanding the target customers that we're selling our products in to. From the standpoint of the employee base, HP, we are big believers of rotations. And so, in our case, we rotate our engineering teams and rather than saying you can sit in Houston and you can design the Notebook and you'll understand exactly what the needs are of some rural farmer in India—umm not a valid assumption. So what we do is we will actually pick up those teams and intersperse them with teams in India and actually design and build products in-country.

So rather than try to do this remotely where someone goes into the field, captures the requirements and brings them back to an engineering team sitting in California or sitting in Texas or Colorado, which is where the three main hubs for our product development occur, we've actually in the last few years shifted to design in-country, build in-country. We did it initially in India. We are now doing it in China and in Brazil, where we actually take teams and station them and intermix them with local teams where the design effort, the manufacturing effort, everything is done in-country. Then those teams come back or we'll take members of the India team and then we'll use that really as a way to address some of the cultural gaps. It's hard to deal with the cultural gaps simply by trying to do it by phone. It does require that face time. Halo [HP's high-end video conferencing system] allows us not to have to get on airplanes nearly as much, but I am a firm believer that the people building the products or people working as teams need to be teams in the field versus isolated teams stuck within organizations."

As a co-activating leader, Phil knows that cultural differences require more than just lip service. In the case of HP, cultural differences are front and center for the head of innovation and play a role not only for employees but also for customers alike. Therefore, as a co-activating leader Phil employs *cultural bonding* to overcome gaps and produce great products while building a leadership arena in which people develop strong social networks that they can leverage no matter where they are, or when they are, in their career.

A case in point is the story of interns with whom Phil is closely involved. Phil employs a co-activating leadership practice that he calls *reverse-mentoring* to keep himself in synch with upcoming youth. We asked him

(continued)

how he knows success has been achieved when developing future leaders using these kinds of collaborations.

"Well, it's kind of interesting. So all three of the interns we hired that year we kept on the payroll through that school year. They went back to their respective schools. So we actually dispersed the team. So albeit Sam was a junior that year, going back as a junior to his school. He was assigned to the HP gaming division. So he ended up working out his school schedule so he didn't have classes on Fridays and Mondays and HP would literally fly him to gaming events. So he was actually on the road representing HP at gaming conferences and being there, doing booth duty at trade shows, those kinds of things.

Michael we hired, moved him to Calgary to be part of a design team for products out of our Calgary group. So he got dropped right into a group that's away from headquarters. Not part of a design team or product team here in headquarters. Joe went back to his west coast university to work on his business degree. We had him doing some business plans, et cetera. And then for year two, Michael had actually graduated, we hired him. Sam and Joe had not graduated, but we brought them back. My rule is that you can't intern in my team two years in a row. So they have to intern in another part of HP if they come back for a second round of internships. That also helps them build out their social networks.

In the case of Michael, we also shipped him to Taiwan for four months as part of the effort to get him rounded out. So here's a kid out of college, barely out college; we hired him, we dropped him to Calgary and then we turn around and we shipped him to Taiwan for four months. So he can build up his relationships and his social network with the Taiwan team, which is critical. Because if you don't have a relationship with the Taiwan team, your ability to design a product and have that product actually go through the manufacturing process is pretty limited.

In the case of those people, also we assigned them region mentors, so people in Taiwan who know the entire process working with Michael to make sure he got the opportunity to touch and be a part of the entire process. So again, it gets back to, it is about face time.

But once you get that face time, use those people to be the new face time that you put out into the regions so that your message gets spread and that those social networks get built up. You can't, you know I can't have a social network where I've got a direct link with 310,000 employees. But within the team that I try to drive and influence, I need to make sure that I've got the strongest possible network such that when I do need to engage those teams they feel like they can be part of the team. It isn't just because it's me as an executive telling them that we need to go do something."

Phil adds to his co-activating leader style by sharing his vision with others and then sending them on their way to experience a wide array of cultures and environments so that they will end up building great products for the company.

To do this Phil leverages his *leader intent;* sharing his knowledge, understanding, and experience along with his vision for the future. But after that, individuals have to rely on their own interpretation of that intent and become leaders in their own right in whatever situation or location they find themselves in. Phil is actively engaged in the process of developing new hires, the new hire is actively engaged in his new experiences, and together they become co-activating leaders co-existing on a leadership continuum at HP.

Phil McKinney represents a leader who has both formal power and informal influence over others. Insights inspired by spending time with younger generations help him both to learn from and manage the best and the brightest. But not all leaders can leverage formal power status. In fact, in the virtual workforce informal influence is of higher value in reducing Virtual Distance, as well as enhancing innovation, and performance. And while many have espoused the virtues of using influence through indirect relationships, never before has this been more important.

The virtual workforce is in fact a loosely coupled set of people who perform best when their contribution, not their formal status, which is often quite meaningless in team and other group efforts, is what they are known for best. In the Virtual Distance Model this aspect of acquiring respect from others is part of Affinity Distance and more specifically we call this factor Social Distance. Recognizing someone based on their contribution status can lower Social Distance, and therefore overall Virtual Distance, to improve outcomes.

But motivating others when you have no formal authority over them is at best difficult without specific effort given to the task. This challenge became more prevalent with the proliferation of matrixed organizations. But the virtual nature of the workforce amplifies this "responsibility with no authority" issue beyond what most people could have imagined. Even with formal authority, motivating those made separate by screens and other social circumstance is not easy.

Co-activating leaders who use informal influence to inspire others to act at all levels in the organization are needed. They play a pivotal role in moving the virtual workforce to action.

Case Two: Making the Most of Motivation at AT&T

Kathy Burke-Thomas is an Associate Director in AT&T's Project Management Center of Excellence, an organization supporting over 10,000 project managers across the globe. Kathy has been with the company for over 25 years, having spent the past ten years developing other people. She is well versed in the trials and tribulations of having moved from traditional employee groups to the dizzying array of virtual workforce designs.

> "We're responsible for supporting people who are project managers and program managers throughout the entire company. And so we offer a variety of training classes and consulting and evaluation tools and different ways to help our project managers build their own personal capabilities and also be more successful with their teams. I put together a class on managing virtual teams. It's built on managing project teams but in particular on how to help influence those over whom we have no formal authority and whom we may never meet.
>
> So a key part of my role is to help others understand how to make things happen given that there may not be any formal link between team members. And a lot of what shapes the way I look at things

has to do with what I learned in the nonprofit and volunteer world. Where you absolutely have no control over people and if you make them mad, they're just going to cross your meeting right off their list."

Kathy, like many other leaders, uses influence to get things done. She understands that she is part of an enterprise ecosystem, one in which there are always people above, below, and next to her.

She has to be able to co-actively work with each group to meet her goals. Among other skills, Kathy uses *360-degree vision* to identify and engage other leaders.

"In the position I'm in right now, I spend about a third of my time managing up (talking to my leadership), a third with my peers in more of a support role because they are doing similar work to what I'm doing, and about a third with the people on the project teams I'm managing. So I have to be aware of how I frame my message and to what audience. You're always going to have a variety of audiences that you're trying to convince and motivate. Especially in project management and particularly with virtual teams.

Our project teams are the ones getting the work done and we want to keep them progressing. And we have to do that not only by helping them to be clear on and having them agree on what it is they're doing and the timeframe they're doing it in. But we also have to try to protect their time by not overwhelming them with a bunch of needless meetings. I really am a big advocate of trying to have people limit the amount of e-mail that they send out because we get in a mode a lot of times having a CYA approach to e-mail. And I just think that's a huge waste of the time for the people on my team.

I'm communicating with them about the things that are pretty clearly laid out in our schedules, but I'm also communicating with my leadership. Because as a project manager I have to keep an eye on the risks that are out there and I have to escalate things. If I can't address them myself, I have to escalate them. I have to manage my relationships with the stakeholders who have an interest in the project."

(continued)

> Kathy adapts her communication style to align with audience prefer-
> ence. And some of the stakeholders are invisible to her in many respects. In
> this way she employs *adaptive communication* knowing exactly with whom
> she is speaking and to what end she wants the conversation to go. Using
> this mechanism Kathy motivates other leaders no matter if they are above
> her, below her, or right alongside her.

Kathy is an experienced communicator who knows that without formal authority, using influence as her main mechanism for motivating
others, she is responsible for ensuring that projects at AT&T are successful. Like many of the leaders discussed so far in this book, Kathy realizes
that the way in which this is done virtually is much different than when
it's done face-to-face.

Yet influencing people in the virtual workforce is a topic that has
gotten very little attention in business schools and other professional
development arenas. One of the most highly cited leadership authors
is a man by the name of Gary Yukl. In his classic work *Leadership in
Organizations,* he describes the importance of oral communications:

> Oral communication allows the effect of words to be magnified by the ef-
> fect of intonation, gestures, and other nonverbal communication. Face-
> to-face interaction facilitates influence attempts and provides an op-
> portunity to obtain immediate feedback about their effectiveness. This
> feedback can be used to modify and improve the manager's influence
> strategy and negotiating effectiveness. The descriptive research found
> that a manager's oral interactions tend to include a surprising amount
> of kidding, joking, and discussing of subjects unrelated to the work (e.g.,
> sports, hobbies) or of trivial importance to it. This socializing activity
> and small talk probably helps managers to build and maintain effective
> relationships with the large network of people whose cooperation and
> support are needed.[2]

But the reality is that almost everything about the way leaders communicate has changed with only episodic exceptions. Coupled with the
fact that most virtual workforce members need to take on leadership
roles from time to time, it's unfathomable to think that the old adage,

"the medium is the message" does not begin to play a major and transformative role in the very underpinnings of many leadership models described by Yukl and others. And yet, here we are teaching new millennium students with the same textbooks using the same leadership theories we've been using for almost a century, when indeed, at the heart of all, sit assumptions about communication effectiveness that are based in whole or in large part on face-to-face interactions. And this just isn't the case anymore.

In addition, securing time from those who won't necessarily realize any financial or related benefit is a major challenge. Influencing such people takes incredible ingenuity from leaders that have an intrinsic sense of how to get people to volunteer. But those qualities alone are not enough. Communications have grown so complex and have diverged quite far from the comfortable constructs that we've been taught.

So it takes a wise and skillful leader to step back, keep cobwebs from growing around under their feet, and continuously reassess how to co-activate others when many voices coalesce in the vacuum of the virtual workforce.

Case Three: Leader Inspiration at NACHRI

Larry McAndrews is the CEO of the National Association of Children's Hospitals and Related Institutions (NACHRI), a nonprofit organization whose mission is to "promote the health and well-being of children and their families through support of children's hospitals and health systems that are committed to excellence in providing health care to children. It does so through advocacy, education, research and health promotion."[3] Co-activating others is a central role in any healthcare environment as the number of relationships and the complexity of the system can be staggering.

"I always enjoyed Peter Drucker who talked about hospitals and characterized them as the most complex organizations in the world. Because you have a customer, the patient, that's served by a third

(continued)

party, the physician that is not controlled by the organization, and paid for by another party, the insurer, with life and death decisions and many different regulators overseeing what you do. So I think that may carry over into our efforts to try to serve them."

Given the challenge of Larry's work of supporting hospitals and advocating for children's well-being, we asked him about some of the communication issues he faces in the digital age.

"As a general philosophy, I believe in being open—if we're all working towards common goals it's important that we all are able to operate with similar information. There are some confidential things, but on the whole most things need to be shared. I think to communicate successfully it's become a lot more complicated, a lot more difficult because you've got so many different things going on.

I think you need to move people away from feeling they are in a passive role and expecting to be given the right information especially when there is so much information coming from everywhere; from the cell phone to the desktop. Everyone needs to be more proactive; positioning themselves as active participants, getting the information they need and making their needs known within the system."

What Larry describes is the need for individuals to become *self-activating leaders*. But Larry knows this is not possible without a strong leader's co-active participation.

"For me, a leader in the context of our organization is a person, through his/her own gifts, working with others, being able to anticipate and position the organization to successfully overcome whatever challenges are on the horizon and to run an organization that people feel good about working for and are enthused and feel stable in enough to provide a service and a product that's useful and helpful to others.

As we have tried to be better and better we have focused more on the particularity of our membership groups and developed a unique set of services for each of the groups, unfortunately that generates more to communicate in the system. As you take on more and more issues and try to fit them into your organizational construct, you get more difficulty and tension in what to communicate. So there's no perfect way to manage this. My thinking on how to proceed in this circumstance is to explain to the staff so they understand that this is the environment that we're currently working within.

So one thing is to get an intellectual understanding and an awareness of the tensions that we have within the organization and then speak openly about those, trying to understand the challenges they bring and develop approaches to overcome those challenges.

We have work groups that work toward separate ends with different rhythms meeting different needs. My sense is to allow enough variability within the organization to optimize the work groups, configuring our policies to make them most effective versus striving for singularity in our approach."

Larry co-activates his staff to help solve multi-faceted problems in an environment that in and of itself is one of the most complex systems in the world, the healthcare system. He doesn't share leadership per se. He remains the person that is responsible to the board and ultimately to the members they serve. However he extends his reach by taking on the role of *co-active enabler;* collaborating with and encouraging others to lead within their own separate but linked spheres.

Though Kathy, Phil, and Larry come from very different organizations, their approach to getting others in the virtual workplace motivated and activated have a lot of common threads. All three recognize that technology has significantly changed the way we communicate and that the overwhelming amount of communication that one receives on any given day can blur away the demarcations of what's really important.

They all know that to succeed in the Digital Age, they need to motivate others to act despite never-ending distractions and do this in a way that differs from traditional management techniques. By co-activating others, they increase their own leadership span while allowing others to grow and develop as well as become leaders in their own right, with or without formal authority to do so. In so doing they leverage the very real and forceful dynamics of informal networks that pervade virtual workspaces.

CONCLUSION

Getting others to volunteer their time is not easy. In today's workplace people are more stretched than ever. Yet, being a co-activating leader involves just that—motivating and inspiring others to do something for the organization without the benefit of any reward and most of the time, without the benefit of establishing face-to-face contact. This lack of a social payoff makes the job of a leader responsible for a virtual workforce even more challenging than ever because social factors, like those described by Yukl, are often those most coveted by other human beings.

But in the virtual workforce there is another way to deliver social benefit and that's to reduce Virtual Distance. Establishing co-active relationships to develop other leaders and then releasing them into their own social networks to build new leader arenas significantly reduces Virtual Distance.

Through cultural bonding and playing the role of global experience advocate, co-activating leaders naturally reduce the negative side effects of Physical Distance. By fanning the desire to become a self-activating leader, effective digital-age leaders help people to feel confident about reducing Operational Distance. Co-activating leaders decrease the daily "noise in the system" and take responsibility for being proactive about solving problems—with or without formal authority. And perhaps most importantly, co-activating leaders significantly reduce Affinity Distance. By creating a sense of shared future and fate the co-activating leader reduces attenuated or absent feelings of interdependence. In addition, through co-activation a person begins to feel that the leader shares their values even though they may never meet. One doesn't choose someone for a position of higher influence, like that of a co-activating leader, unless they have similar values around work and a genuine respect for others. And, finally, a team member knows that their contributions matter because co-activating new leaders wouldn't encourage them to lead if what they themselves did wasn't seen as important.

All of this leads to greater trust, higher levels of satisfaction, and better citizenry behavior. In addition, higher levels of motivation to volunteer time, energy, and resources to forward organizational goals are gained. This can all occur even when people rarely or even never meet. Reducing Virtual Distance is *the big bang for the buck* that people intuitively respond to—it's rewarding to be happier and truly engaged in the virtual workforce.

NOTES

1. S. Palmisano, "The Globally Integrated Enterprise," *Foreign Affairs* (May/June 2006) Vol. 85 No. 3.
2. G. Yukl, *Leadership in Organizations* 5th Edition (Upper Saddle River, NJ: Prentice-Hall, 2002).
3. Mission statement of NACHRI retrieved from www.nachri.org

6

Techno-Dexterity

I t may be hard for some younger readers to believe but there was a time when no Internet, e-mail, instant messaging, voice mail, wireless, or PDAs even existed. When five o'clock rolled around you were finished with work for the day and when you started the next morning you didn't have a hundred e-mails to read. It's a wonder to marvel at the speed with which technology has created a new kind of work life, often indistinguishable from our non-working life. On the plus side, technology enables us to work any time and from almost anywhere. On the negative side, technology enables us to work any time and from almost anywhere. Technology, as all of us know, can be both a blessing and a curse.

One of the central theses of this book is that effective leaders in virtual environments must acquire new skills not yet highlighted or discussed in any of the existing leadership models. The most successful of today's leaders understand how to use technology in a more socially adapted way to impart vision and inspire others. This skill is called **techno-dexterity** because it involves an understanding of and competence in using the right technology to successfully convey the right message. The technology comes in different forms and can be applied in different ways to help build the three pillars of virtual leadership discussed thus far: **creating context**, **building and cultivating communities**, and **co-activating new leadership**.

E-MAIL

In the first book, *Uniting the Virtual Workforce*, the problems of e-mail—the sheer volume, the ambiguous norms about responding, and the difficulty of clearly communicating what we intend to communicate, were discussed in detail.[1] One of the leaders that we interviewed has met these challenges in an interesting way.

On Fridays, Robert McMahon, President of U.S. Commercial Operations at Merck & Co., Inc., routinely drives from his home in Pennsylvania to his summer home on Long Island and then back on Sunday. It's a long drive. Bob's wife drives both ways enabling him to get some work done.

> I'll sit in the passenger seat on my computer and get three or four hours of work done. What I won't do is be online when I do that. What I'll do is package up all those messages because I can work offline and wait until I know everybody's gone to bed on Sunday night and then get on line and release them all. Rather than having messages straggling in over the weekend and people saying, oh, the son of a gun is online again, I'm running for the hills, what they get is a sense of is he's not online or he's not working, but I've bundled all of what I needed to do in a way that doesn't interfere with peoples' space on the weekend. And then it arrives when they arrive in the office on Monday morning. It looks like all hell broke loose about 10:03 on a Sunday night.

Working offline shows respect for the dividing line between work and non-work, relieving McMahon's employees from the dilemma of whether an e-mail received on Saturday or Sunday needs an immediate response. By using traditional e-mail strategically, he reinforces the validity of downtime and establishes a sense of continuity among his people.

Certainly, creating and maintaining a vision is one of the most important aspects of leadership. But how do you do it when your employees are spread all over the country? In McMahon's case about 97 percent of his employees are outside the headquarters building in Pennsylvania. Video mail is another solution.

> I think the big jump for me within the last couple years are video mails. Where I would do a four or five minute, maybe sometimes a little bit longer video mail; talk about an aspect of the strategy with some slides flashing up on the screen as I'm talking. That adds maybe some news to where we're headed, updates them, refreshes them on why we're doing what we're doing. The video mail is accompanied by an ability for them to provide feedback and ask questions. It has free text in it. So it has some pre-positioned questions and then I get to see in the aftermath of the video mail how they, in an anonymous way, how they reacted to it, how they viewed it. So I did one that was viewed by over 3,000 people within three days who provided over 500 individual pieces of feedback, which somebody on this end synthesized for me and gave me the output from the questions that we sent. I then turned around with their help back to my leadership team and said, here's what I heard when this message went out. You need to help me with x, y, and z. Here's what I'm going to do next. And they know what my communication intent is in terms of subsequent videos or appearances or whatever. So, it is a very good way of communicating and learning and for then re-communicating. And the anonymity of it, in a sense, is very powerful.

Because he knows how to use old and new technologies effectively, with dexterity, Bob's leadership lessens Virtual Distance and broadens his **commitment to community**.

TELECONFERENCING

Like video mails, teleconferencing adds social presence to communications. We can talk to one another, give immediate feedback and reach consensus. But teleconferencing has its limits especially as the group gets larger. Hewlett Packard's Phil McKinney points to another problem with conference calls,

> The fact is, that we all tend to fall into kind of our conference call discussion mode. Somebody's talking, you find it very hard to interject or actually have a two-way dialogue, so you go into pause and wait mode. Wait until someone pauses and then you say—I've got a point or—I've got a question.

We've all been on conference calls where the participation is uneven. We may not even be sure that the other person is listening, instead answering e-mail or taking another call, perhaps. We've also seen the problem with a lack of engagement on the part of some participants when teams are a mix of cultures and languages. Jessica Lipnack, a pioneer in virtual teams and CEO of NetAge, recognizes the issues.

> We know that if you only have a conference call, what are people going to do? Their e-mail, their bills; they'll do anything but pay attention.

Lipnack says that a "focusing mechanism" is needed to overcome these limitations. One of the ways to focus participants is to have a shared screen. This gives everyone some shared context for the discussion and Lipnack says leads to a more successful interaction. But even with shared screens, interactions in conference calls tend to be strictly task-focused with little room for building relationships. The limited social presence and high physical distance make it difficult for people to interact in ways that can help build friendships and trust.

However, AT&T's Kathy Burke-Thomas provided an interesting example of how you can use conferencing technology to maintain social relationships.

> One person on my team asked if we could have a virtual lunch together. So what we do is we schedule a time just like we would if we were in the same city. We schedule a time on our calendars and she always includes her picture even though I know good and well what she looks like. We'll kind of set the ground rules, like ten minutes to talk about work. We started this with a few of us who are on the same team and I don't really know what inspired us to start it. I think it was one was in Chicago, one's

in St. Louis, and I'm in Kansas City. We just wanted to have a little bit more personal time because we really liked getting to talk to each other. And then, one person moved to a different organization and we kept the virtual lunches going just because it's a way to network and kind of keep tabs on what's going on in other groups. And I would say that it has helped us to weather those times when there might have been a little more friction within our virtual team. If we had been in the same city, I don't know that I would have followed through on going out to lunch every time. But because we'd made the commitment, we would do it and I just think that it's really made a big difference. It's helped out a lot.

Despite its limitations, then, teleconferencing can be made more effective when leaders focus the participants with a shared screen, for example, or introduce a social presence into the event. Successful leaders push technology to its limits to produce the maximum benefit for all concerned and nowhere is that more apparent than with teleconferencing.

VIDEO CONFERENCING

Of course, one alternative to voice teleconferencing is video. We've come a long way since the early days of cumbersome video conferencing systems. Here's Lipnack's description of an international video conference at a large pharmaceutical company.

> You couldn't even see the people on the screen. It was completely ridiculous. You could barely hear them, you couldn't see them. You couldn't see the documents that we wanted to work on. So video conferencing was very poorly used, very poorly regarded by the teams that we surveyed; however, that's going to change very rapidly because we now have compression algorithms that make it possible to get very high resolution bandwidth pictures being transmitted; however, there's always going to be a limitation to how many faces you can get on a screen.

Most of the executives that we interviewed agreed that video adds something very important to a teleconference. Jack Barsky,

Vice President of Information Technology at energy giant NRG, for example, told us:

> It's vastly superior to just teleconferencing. When you see the other person, it makes a big difference. I have one direct report who is normally in Texas. Three out of four weeks, she's down there and she lives there. And of the other direct reports, typically one of them is on the road. So when I have my staff meetings, there are usually two of them in the same room or in different rooms, but not here. Yet we can see one another. Somehow it works so much better than when people are dialed in. You don't have the visual clues, if you're on the phone, you just don't have the same attention. You don't give as much attention to that meeting. You have a tendency to drift off because you're just not there.

Barsky's comments point to how increasing social presence can lead to increased attention and increased engagement. Even fairly inexpensive video connections can be quite effective in creating a sense of presence and shared context. And the technology is getting better all the time.

Phil McKinney's team in HP's Innovation Program is spread all over the globe. Phil has made good use of HP's Video Conferencing solution.

> When you're in the room [Halo], literally within about five minutes, you forget the fact that you're in a room and that the people that you're looking at on the other side of the table are 3,000 miles away. And you can have a fully natural conversation. You know, we go into extreme situations where we have spatial audio so if you're sitting in a room and I'm facing people across, on the monitors on the other side of the room. And these are high definition, 1080p high def signals coming both directions, and somebody on the far side of the other room talks, I hear it from that side of the room as if I was sitting in the room. So it's not just the video, it's not just the audio; it's the whole sensory side of it. The rooms themselves are designed so that the walls are not square. The walls actually come in to give you a sense of perspective so that you look more 3-D versus kind of flat against a flat wall, sitting at a table. So it's all of that in order to give you a sense that you're actually sitting in the room and you quickly fall into just this natural ability to have conversation versus the video and audio technologies that are out there today.

And the one side benefit is that two years ago I did 240,000 miles in the air. Last year I did about 130,000 and this year I don't think I'm going to break 70,000 miles in the air. And I think the results from the teams have significantly improved. In addition, we do this with customers too. I've got customers in New York who I meet with on a regular basis and instead of getting on an airplane and them going on an airplane, they get in their cab, they go over to our Penn Station HP Office, which is where our Halo suite is in Manhattan. They walk into that room; I walk into the room just on the other side of my office here in California. We do a two-hour meeting, we're done. They get to have lunch in New York and I start my day here in California.

What you find in Halo, and part of the secret in Halo's research that came out of HP labs where we recognized that there was a certain conversation style when people could actually see people, one. But, also, there's a tight, tight synchronization between the video and the audio. So if we're sitting in the room, there's no delay between the movement of your lips and the audio I hear. And we can have a natural flow of conversation. There's no delay.

The advantage of this sophisticated technology over e-mail, video mail, and teleconferencing is obvious, but it also saves costs, wear and tear on managers, and helps to reinforce **co-operative communities**. However, it can't completely replace face-to-face meetings because Virtual Distance would then widen and negate its purpose. Maintaining this balance between technology and human interaction is the challenge faced by every contemporary leader.

SOCIAL NETWORK TECHNOLOGY

We all get them. E-mails telling us that so and so wants to link up with us on some social networking site. Danah Boyd and Nicole Ellison[2] study these sites, which they define as "web-based services that allow individuals to (1) construct a public or semi-public profile within a bounded system, (2) articulate a list of other users with whom they share a connection, and (3) view and traverse their list of connections and those made by others within the system."

What makes social network sites unique is not that they allow individuals to meet strangers, but rather that they enable users to articulate and make visible their existing social networks. This can result in connections between individuals that would not otherwise be made, but that is often not the goal, and these meetings are frequently between "latent ties" who share some offline connection. On many of the large social network sites (SNS), participants are not necessarily "networking" or looking to meet new people; instead, they are primarily communicating with people who are already a part of their extended social network.

As Boyd and Ellison point out, the history of social network sites began in 1997 with Six Degrees.com and progressed relatively slowly until Facebook and LinkedIn were introduced in 2003. As of this writing, LinkedIn claims to have more than 30 million registered users from 122 different industries.

In one sense, networks are communities of common interest that can be useful for job seekers or keeping in touch with colleagues. There does not seem to be any real thought to using networks for purposes of leadership. We asked all of our interviewees how they used social network technology and got a range of responses. Some leaders make little or no use of these sites but others have figured out how to use them in creative ways. One example was described by Guido Petit. In his role as leader of the Alcatel-Lucent Technical Academy, Guido wanted to connect technical experts within the company.

> But how to do that? Of course, in the past it was decided to set up a database with the names and the competencies and skills of all the technical experts in the company. The only problem that we faced was that such a database needs to be kept up-to-date, central, and yet able to convince the people to update their competencies, and their skills themselves. But if they don't get it finished or when they change jobs and they forget to update their profile, then all information is outdated and you know what happens with a database with outdated information, people are using it once, people are using it twice, but the third time they say, well look, I don't find the experts because the information is outdated. And they are not going to use the tool anymore. So we said we

have to come up with another alternative. And the other alternative was very simple.

Guido took up a proposal to set up a bulletin board where anybody in the company could post a request for help. The help could come in the form of a technical expert, someone who could answer a technical question from a customer or almost anything. The question is posted by the requestor on the bulletin board and then the Academy takes it as a challenge to connect the requestor in 24 hours with somebody who has the technical expertise to help the person. Guido says,

> So we are not looking for big technical experts or the top technical expert, no, we are looking for somebody who has the technical expertise and the willingness to answer the question of the requestor. So we connect people. And it was a very simple tool, low effort because the bulletin board is a tool that exists. And the other thing that we needed to do as soon as the request has been posted, is to broadcast it to the ALTA members and we have a community of 500 ALTA members and they are using their network internally or externally to find a person willing to connect with the requestor and to answer the technical question. So it is connecting experts, it is sharing information, we do it in 24 hours and we are using the network of technical experts inside the company. And that is improving directly or indirectly also the R&D effectiveness because when doing a study on your own, you first check whether the study has been done in the company and most likely somebody in the company has done the same technical study for maybe customer A or customer B. So if you don't ask, you probably are going to start that work again and that will take you weeks perhaps. Now, you first launch the request figuring out who has done such a study in the past, what was the result, and then you can decide if you need to do some extra work or if you can re-use the result for the project you are working in.

The core group of Alcatel-Lucent Technical Academy members meet face-to-face in several ways. First, there is an annual meeting where Academy members get together for recognition and also have a chance to meet and socialize. Second, the Academy is divided into regional chapters which hold meetings more frequently. Finally, the experts identified through the bulletin board get together face-to-face in working sessions. Guido estimated that 80,000 people in the company worldwide are connected through the bulletin board.

Gina Poole, Vice President of Software Group Marketing 2.0 at IBM knows more than a little about social network technology. Part of her mission at IBM is to promote and facilitate the use of social software tools to help teams be more productive and effective. One question that intrigued us is whether social network technology can really be used to build long-distance relationships. As she was building her team, Gina was on the lookout for talented people who could help her in her mission. She told us an interesting story about meeting an IBM employee who lives on a remote island and connects to the rest through a virtual social network.

> He is the only IBMer living there. He doesn't go into an office and network with colleagues. But he is incredibly active in our social networks across the company, as well as externally. Before he worked for me, everywhere I turned, I'd bump into him online, or people would say, "Oh social networking—have you talked with Luis?" So here's a guy sitting in the middle of an ocean, but he is incredibly well-known in the social networks inside and outside IBM. I had him come to Orlando for a conference and as he and I were walking around, people were recognizing him and hugging him. He is a great example of someone who builds relationships online and offline.

Paul Levy is the President and CEO of Beth Israel Deaconess Medical Center in Boston, not someone you would expect to be on Facebook. But Levy began using Facebook a few years ago to build a community, not just for those in the hospital or health care but also for the broader community. His Facebook group is open to everyone. Levy uses his Facebook connections to schedule events where people get together for some face-to-face social activities. Among the events that Levy has scheduled with his Facebook group:

- Inviting people to the hospital cafeteria for a free healthy snack (admission is a printout of their invitation on Facebook)

- Bringing a harpist to play music in the cafeteria for another session where healthy snacks are served
- A cruise for Facebook friends in Boston Harbor
- A private tour of Fenway Park

Levy builds his community with social network technology and then closes the Virtual Distance gap by having fun, social events with the members.[3] He then leverages the network by doing things like raising money for a hospital in Gabon, Africa.

All three of the examples of social networks have two things in common. First, the network is built virtually by using technology around some common purpose or sense of community and second, all three combine face-to-face meetings to reduce the physical, operational, and affinity distance between those in the network.

BLOGS

Weblogs, or as they are commonly known, blogs, have emerged in the past decade as a vehicle for quickly communicating information and opinion to a wider audience. Several of the senior leaders we spoke to contribute regularly to their own blogs.

As Gina Poole told us, blogging is a staple activity at IBM. Gina is both a blogger and a reader of blogs. In addition she uses blogs to learn about potential contributors, extend her social network, as well as recruit participants for her virtual team projects.

Phil McKinney told us how he used his blog to talk about a ***reverse mentoring*** program in which he invited several college students to stay with him for the summer while they worked at HP. Here is how McKinney describes reverse mentoring on his blog.

> Hanging out with staff and interns that are younger than your own children is a real eye-opener. You quickly realize that you are so far out of the loop—you can't even see the loop. The challenge is how do you get yourself back into the loop without looking like an old guy trying to re-live your childhood or worse—going through your midlife crisis by "hanging out." In my case, I have three summer interns who are quite

diverse in their backgrounds and degrees. One is an industrial/graphic designer, another a business major and the third is a computer science major. One is from outside the United States, the others come from each coast. Now that's what I call diversity! My goal with interns is to not only give them experience, skills, and mentoring that they will find beneficial as they get ready to launch their careers—but to also learn from them. It's what I call "reverse mentoring."[4]

More recently, McKinney used his blog to discuss a museum exhibit of Leonardo da Vinci's notebooks and used the example to highlight the importance of capturing ideas in notebooks for innovation.

The heading of Paul Levy's blog states, "This is a blog started by a CEO of a large Boston Hospital to share thoughts about hospitals, medicine, and health care issues."[5] In fact, his blog does all that and more covering a wide range of topics including his thoughts about management, leadership, and social issues. In one blog entry, Levy, under the heading "Do I get paid too much?" disclosed his compensation and invited feedback from his readers.

VIRTUAL WORLDS

Virtual worlds are older than you might think. In the 1960s Morton Heilig patented an immersive virtual reality technology called Sensorama. Sensorama was able to create stereoscopic 3-D film images in a wide-angle view, had stereo sound, and even provided odors.[6] Sensorama was a fairly limited mechanical device and though ingenuous, never went much further than a prototype.

Today, we can easily access a variety of immersive virtual worlds on the Internet. Virtual worlds are web-based simulated environments in which avatars, representing users, interact with other avatars, which may represent other users or may be simulations. Virtual worlds include a broad array of applications such as Second Life.

Piet Hut is a world-renowned astrophysicist at the Institute for Advanced Study in Princeton, New Jersey, who discovered Second Life after experimenting with a few other virtual worlds. He began building communities there and describes how one of the communities took hold.

> We got a number of serious amateurs and professional computer scientists interested in helping astronomy. It's called the Meta Institute for Computational Astrophysics or MICA and it really took off in Second Life. For a half a year, we had a weekly board meeting. I wrote the agenda and the minutes and we had 10–15 people and it slowly started growing. Half astronomers and half Second Lifers working together setting up working groups. We had professional talks, general talks, popular talks. We had all kinds of events like "ask an astronomer." People could ask questions about the big bang. People love that.

Piet's experience serves as an illustration as to how one can use this new medium to build communities around common interests. And business organizations are using Second Life, as well. Gina Poole, for example, told us that she uses Second Life to help build and maintain her community of BlueIQ Ambassadors—the folks that volunteer to help her with her mission of promoting and enabling the use of social software tools. In addition, Cisco Systems has been hosting virtual meetings on Second Life for a couple of years now.

Will Second Life or other virtual social worlds become one of the technological tools used by leaders? Some are pessimistic, citing the difficulty of learning how to use the Second Life technology and frustration with the interface.[7] On the other hand, Ned Kock, a leading expert in the area of virtual collaboration notes that early experiments in E-learning experienced similar problems. He says,

> Many of the problems with early online courseware suites were interface related, and some of those problems led to dire predictions about the demise of online instruction and of the companies behind it.[8]

CONCLUSION

The successful leaders interviewed understand **techno-dexterity** and how to exploit technology to create and maintain the three pillars of virtual leadership: **context**, **community**, and **co-activating leaders**.

Context

To create, maintain, and deepen context, these leaders use e-mail with video or audio to make organizational vision more salient and powerful. By adding shared screens to teleconferencing, they enable participants to focus on a common reference point, thus increasing shared context. With high definition video conference systems, they increase social presence. Visualizing facial expressions and body language allows for immediate feedback and promotes common perspective among participants regardless of location. While blogs enrich context through a common framework that promotes the flow of ideas, strengthening communication between team members.

Community

To build and maintain communities, leaders set aside time for social teleconferences in which participants nourish relationships vital to a group identity. Utilizing video conferencing maintains and extends connections formed from face-to-face meetings, evoking more attached emotional responses than those provided by e-mail or voice alone. Social networking technology fosters connections between people who already share a community of interest. Blogs allow us to create connections with individuals of like interests, while virtual social worlds like Second Life offer communities a virtual context in which to additionally sustain themselves.

Co-Activating New Leaders

All of these technologies, when used with dexterity, produce opportunities for co-activating new leaders. Social networks help initiate and maintain relationships with potential leaders for specific projects or initiatives, especially those undertaken on a voluntary basis. Teleconferencing with shared screens and video conferencing allows each member to take a lead role for specific subtasks. Blogs provide information for those who might serve as leaders for specific initiatives, with virtual social worlds allowing individuals to become leaders in communities built around common themes or interests.

NOTES

1. K. Sobel Lojeski, R. Reilly, *Uniting the Virtual Workforce: Transforming Leadership and Innovation in the Globally Integrated Enterprise* (Hoboken, NJ: John Wiley & Sons, 2008)

2. D.M. Boyd, and N.B. Ellison, "Social Network Sites: Definition, History, and Scholarship," *Journal of Computer-Mediated Communication* (2007) 13(1), article 11. jcmc.indiana.edu/vol13/issue1/boyd.ellison.html

3. We are indebted to Jessica Lipnack for telling us about her Facebook friend Paul Levy.

4. www.philmckinney.com/blog.html

5. runningahospital.blogspot.com/

6. H. Rheingold, *Virtual Reality: The Revolutionary Technology of Computer-Generated Artificial Worlds—and How It Promises to Transform Society* (New York: Simon & Schuster, 1992).

7. G. Anthes, "Second Life: Is There Any There There?" *Computerworld* (2007) 41(49), 30–38.

8. N. Kock, "E-collaboration and E-commerce in Virtual Worlds: The Potential of Second Life and World of Warcraft," *International Journal of e-Collaboration*, (2008) 4, 1–13.

CHAPTER 7

The Virtual Distance Leadership Model

The leadership crisis described at the outset of this book has arrived over time. In the mid part of the twentieth century most
Americans believed that corporate leaders could be trusted and
that business organizations in general were good for the country. Over
the last 50 years, that sentiment has been changed, if not lost. And
not just in America. People around the globe feel that developing
good leadership in the future may be an elusive and rarely achieved
pursuit.

Much of the concern about leadership stems from the growing divide
between the issues we face today versus the business models created
almost a century ago. When Frederick Winslow Taylor, often referred to
as the father of modern day organizational bureaucracy, espoused the
virtues of scientific management in 1911 with its top-down structures
in which communication was heavily guarded and only flowed in one
direction, the notion of cyber-communication was an idea that even the
most futuristic thinkers hadn't imagined.

As management models evolved there was no consideration of a "virtual team" or other such work groups. Instead academics and organizational behaviorists relied on core assumptions, explicit and implicit, that had team members communicating face-to-face, working in the same office, being of the same ilk, and more. And even though everything about the way we work has changed, these models continue as the mainstays of business school curriculums and corporate training programs. Leadership models derived from the same outdated assumptions also continue to pervade most business books. And for the most part, they are ineffective.

What has not yet been considered is the effect of Virtual Distance—an unintended consequence of widespread electronic communication. As Virtual Distance rises without proper leadership the results can be devastating. Distrust calcifies among virtual resources resulting in lost innovation opportunities and low growth of advanced ideas. In the first book on the subject, detailed accounts of how millions of dollars can be lost as a result of failed projects directly attributable to high levels of Virtual Distance were discussed.[1] Leader effectiveness falls prey to these forces as well. When people perceive themselves to be distant from one another, no matter if it is an unconscious byproduct of the virtual environment, even though they have limitless technical access to each other, a paradox emerges. This is called the **Connectivity Paradox.** When set in motion, leader effectiveness sinks into an abyss of apathy and lack of engagement on the part of followers.

But it doesn't have to be this way. The leaders showcased here demonstrate pro-active behaviors that feed and amplify the development of good relationships, minimizing Virtual Distance. Their actions ultimately unfold into higher levels of performance and greater innovation. What's key is that these leaders realize that many of the old ways don't work anymore, so they've adjusted their thinking and implemented new kinds of leadership behaviors.

THE VIRTUAL DISTANCE LEADERSHIP MODEL

Effective leaders take three actions in particular that help them communicate their vision, inspire others, and motivate people to act. These

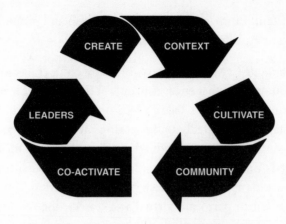

FIGURE 7.1   The Virtual Distance Leadership Model

actions are captured in the Virtual Distance Leadership Model shown in Figure 7.1.

1. Create Context

Virtual workforce leaders create context for those who don't have enough information to make fully informed decisions about others' communications. When things are done mostly face-to-face there is no loss of shared physical context. Shared mental models become evident through conversation and cues like knowing where people live, whom they work for, and what organizations they belong to "outside" of work. Shared views of organizational mission are easily acquired through joint meetings between leaders and followers in a setting conducive to the viral spread of overall goals and objectives. Inspiration comes directly through leaders and managers sitting side by side with employees spurring them to act. Motivation can be fueled by rousing messages delivered by skilled orators and local peer pressure. Vision, mission, inspiration, and enthusiasm grow out of natural organic organizational models that are designed to disseminate the word.

But today this context is often lost amid the intensive eye contact with screens instead of other human beings. It follows that one of the most important things leaders can do is establish and promote context. There are four aspects to context building:

1. *Continuous Cognitive Context.* Building context has to be a continuous process that engages people at the cognitive level. In every meeting, whether it's face-to-face or virtual, leaders need to set the stage by repeatedly underscoring missions and goals. It is in this context that an individual's work is ultimately measured and judged. And it is through these features that people sitting together and worlds apart are connected to the institution. If mission and vision fail to permeate virtual workforces, then individual performance and group work suffers. Cognitive context needs to be constructed under the direction of the leader. If people are physically separated then it's important for the leader to draw a picture for others that captures the places and texture germane to others' locales. And continuously emphasizing others' views of the world through examples of their participation in outside endeavors and other activities helps others understand just where people are coming from. In this way, a shared sense of values—organizational, work, and personal—begin to form.

2. *Contextual Constant.* In the virtual workforce, team members are constantly shifting, as are situations, priorities, and a host of other factors. Team members' attention is often turned in a number of directions. To keep virtual team members pointed properly someone, something, has to be kept constant. The constant is the leader. The leader has to be the anchor—the familiar voice in the dark—when people are working across space, time, and virtual voids.

3. *Comprehensive Context.* To be a stable contextual entity, the leader must bring to bear a lot of information about other people and organizational frameworks. The leader must fully understand the strategic vision and mission as well as translate that to the various virtual workforces. The leader must also have the experience and perspective to provide a context that is broad enough for everyone to share.

4. *Contagious Context*. The leader is the main storyteller in the virtual workforce. She/he must explain organizational matters in a way that sparks positive appeal to the virtual workforce. Without colorful stories that reflect a sense of passion and drive, it would be difficult for others to be motivated enough to move goals forward. The leader must be centered on their mission and transmit an emotional energy to everyone no matter what the communication mode.

Table 7.1 shows how creating context reduces Virtual Distance.

2. Cultivate Community

The notion that strong community building is needed to ensure the health of the enterprise is nothing new. In the mid twentieth century, organizational leaders expected employees to be engaged with their local towns and activities. This solidified an important social relationship needed to bond the organization to society. However, much of that commitment has disappeared as the emphasis has shifted to online relationships that many consider to be disconnected from natural societal ties.

This is a false assumption. The leader discussions highlighted in this book show a clear connection between virtual community building and higher levels of innovation, performance, and leader development at both the local as well as the global level. The key elements of cultivating communities are:

a. *Co-Operative Communities*. Groups in which people do more than simply gather information and learn from one another but go further to self-instigate action on behalf of the group for the betterment of the entire organization.

b. *Constructive Communities*. Groups whose members embody activist energy and fuel further developments by finding ways to *positively* add to the greater good.

TABLE 7.1 Reducing Virtual Distance through Context Building

Creating Context	Physical Distance	Reducing Virtual Distance Through Context Building	
		Operational Distance	Affinity Distance
Continuous Cognitive Context	• Color in background for virtual workforce members reducing negative effects of lack of shared physical spaces. • Illuminate organizations others work for and explain how they relate to other team members reducing organizational distance.	• Create perspective around others' work load, reducing potential multitasking demands • Share information about team members' involvement with organizational mission helping everyone understand communications in their proper frames.	• Provide information about others' mental models helping team members understand how values align. • Help team members interpret similarities between themselves and others to more easily make natural connections and build social capital. • Emphasize contributions from other team members so that formal status differences can be neutralized.
Contextual Constant	• Establish stable leader context across different locations, time zones, organizations • Establish common points of reference • Establish common communication path for complex matters	• Establish common arbiter of priorities • Formulate consistent messages and communication context • Provide reliable syntheses of organizational mission and goals	• Nurture shared trust across the enterprise reducing cultural distance • Show how "weak ties" connect virtual workforce team members reducing relationship distance • Provide focal point for common goals and objectives reducing interdependence distance.

Comprehensive Context	• Provide broad scope and demonstration of experience across multiple locations, time zones, organizations • Fill in gaps for widely separated team members with reliable and trusted experience	• Provide extensive backdrop around communications • Draw on wide array of messages to suit distributed team members • Demonstrate ability to tap resources when needed	• Point to value similarities among broad swath of people • Make introductions to people across varied organizations and locales • Underscore interdependence among many different virtual workforce units
Contagious Context	• Build momentum among distributed workforce • Maintain positive passion regardless of place, time, organizational affiliation	• Frame stories consistently • Increase motivation to work on multiple projects and assignments	• Paint picture of how virtual team members relate to one another • Emphasize commonalities between virtual team members • Relay success stories that reflect positive outcomes in similar work groups

c. *Coherent Communities.* Groups whose members stay with the community consistently over long time periods contributing regularly to the effort.

d. *Confluent Communities.* Groups whose members know what they are charged to do and who clearly and effectively communicate their mission and present their solutions consistently to the outside world. No matter who in the community is asked to represent it at any given point in time, their message and approach are easily associated with other members'.

e. *Community Commitment.* The groups' leader is driven by a long-standing passion to bring disparate groups of people together to act in ways that create new groups who then discover new ways to work and live and inspire others to do the same.

Table 7.2 illustrates how cultivating communities reduces Virtual Distance.

3. Co-Activating New Leaders

Many believe that shared leadership is an important aspect of developing the virtual workforce. While this idea remains one to be considered it was found that the notion of "sharing leadership" deflects thinking in the wrong direction. Instead great leaders activate others to lead and in so doing, fuel their own energies. This dynamic is named co-activating leadership.

Established leaders look for up-and-coming leaders whom they take responsibility for—whether it's a formal requirement or an informal desire to ensure future organizational viability. Instead of thinking about their responsibilities as something to be split up and parsed out, successful leaders seed virtual workers with the knowledge and behavior that enables leadership to flower, recognizing that ultimately, the individual team member will shape their ideals and communications differently.

TABLE 7.2 Reducing Virtual Distance through Cultivating Community

Cultivating Community	Reducing Virtual Distance Through Cultivating Community		
	Physical Distance	Operational Distance	Affinity Distance
Co-Operative Communities	• Tightly integrated shared mission and vision reduces effects of large geographic, time, and organizational distances	• All engaged understand the meaning of what others have to say reducing chances of misunderstanding and conflict	• Goals are aligned and self-enacted keeping people feeling close to one another and motivated to act on behalf of one another
Constructive Communities	• Pervade positive attitudes and respect for one another's time and schedule	• Criticism kept at professional level • Conflict at the personal level is minimized allowing people to share new ideas, innovate on larger scales, and take risks for others	• Members socialize with one another and help new members and/or users of the community get familiar with others keeping social distance to a minimum and extending the ties necessary to keep relationship distance at bay
Confluent Communities	• No matter where the person is, community members all speak the "same language"	• Terms identifying community development activity are understood by all keeping miscommunications to a minimum and enabling maximum use of all communication modes	• Members share direction and approach while adding personal style to fit any given situation allowing for reduced cultural distance and increased stylistic freedom
Community Commitment	• Leader explicitly and demonstrably works to enable virtual as well as face-to-face interactions among distributed community members	• Leader sets the tone for communications and includes the proper context in order to let communication flow easily among members	• Leader helps members to build strong and lasting relationships that matter in a meaningful way to individual members as well as to the overall community

The main features of co-activating new leaders include:

a. *Global Experience Advocacy*. A quality of the co-activating leader that encourages leader development through global experience.

b. *Cultural Bonding*. Co-activating leaders promote the development of teams through direct contact with other people and places in which the team's target product or service will ultimately be delivered. A co-activating leader knows that without this kind of interaction, it would be almost impossible to deliver great products and services without sacrificing value to the target customer.

c. *Reverse Mentoring*. A co-activating leader looks forward to learning from younger generations. They recognize that today's youth have much to teach older, more experienced workers. Therefore the co-activating leader looks to youth to mentor them, and in so doing, they become a co-activating leader with the older person.

d. *Leader Intent*. Co-activating leaders establish a shared experience with their vision and goals that is then carried out through new leaders. Leader intent is key to ensuring that new leaders work in concert with the established leader's vision. However leader intent does not constrict the new leader from shaping and developing his/her own perspective on how to get the job done.

e. *360 Degree Vision*. The co-activating leader knows that in order to influence people they need to understand what all levels of the organization want and need. And this has to be done without necessarily ever being face-to-face with those they need to influence. The co-activating leader needs to keep in mind all of the stakeholders who are affected by his/her decisions.

f. *Adaptive Communication*. The co-activating leader modifies his/her communication style depending on where their audience member sits within a stakeholder network. The co-activating leader takes care not to overburden already harried virtual workers while at the same time managing risk factors important to more senior leadership.

g. *Self-Activating Leaders.* Co-activating leaders understand that they alone cannot provide enough motivation to move virtual workforce members into a leadership role. Virtual workers also have to be self-activating in order to rise to the occasion.

Table 7.3 shows how co-activating leadership reduces Virtual Distance.

THE "HOW" OF VIRTUAL DISTANCE LEADER EXCELLENCE

So far the three main actions taken by great leaders to maximize innovation and performance throughout the virtual workforce have been described; Create Context, Cultivate Community, Co-Activating Leadership. These competencies help to reduce Virtual Distance and therefore improve almost every critical outcome imaginable. *How* great leaders do this varies. However, as shown in Figure 7.2, we discovered four key aspects that are important to emphasize.

1. Techno-Dexterity

Techno-dexterity is a skill that must be developed if leaders expect to be effective. With the many different communication avenues available, a leader must know when to use what, with whom, and how to make every communication as valuable as possible. When leaders are considering their options it's important they think about the following:

a. Is the message likely to contain information that will cause an emotional reaction that might be difficult to deal with? If the answer is yes, then a face-to-face meeting or a phone call should be used. It's important not to leave people hanging in virtual spaces if it's likely they'll need to ask questions in real time as information is provided.

b. Would personal emphasis be particularly helpful to get the message across? If the answer is yes then a venue suited to support as many

TABLE 7.3 Reducing Virtual Distance through Co-Activating Leaders

Co-Activating New Leaders	Reducing Virtual Distance Through Co-Activating Leaders		
	Physical Distance	Operational Distance	Affinity Distance
Co-activating Leadership	• Co-activating leaders mix face time with screen time reducing the negative impacts of high physical distance	• Co-activating leaders strive to create cross-communication among other future leaders within the context of shared development	• Co-activating leaders inherently nurture links between cultural values, interdependence, social ties and a respect for someone's contribution versus their status
Global Experience Advocate	• Global experience by definition calls for people to spend time in the field and get face time with others who are geographically dispersed	• Global experience helps people to internalize the way others communicate, and in what context they work, live, and view the world. This lessens context gaps and heightens the value of virtual communications when face time is not available	• Global experience helps people to understand each other in terms of value systems closing the chasm on this most insidious distance–causing factor. Establishing social ties with others while in their locale helps to cement long term relationships
Cultural Bonding	• Co-activating leaders encourage living in the shoes of others by being physically close and teamed together locally	• Co-activating leaders know that language and context barriers are erased when cultural bonding takes place hastening fluidity of communications in the short and long term	• Co-activating leaders can be sure to reap the rewards of cultural bonding when people develop deep appreciation for others' life circumstances bringing all closer together

Reverse Mentoring	• Co-activating leaders realize that creating immersive face-time experiences where younger workers mentor experienced workers brings everyone closer together	• Co-activating leaders know that their communication approach as compared with younger people is going to be very different and reverse mentoring, youth teaching the older generations, helps to reduce communication issues and make context more available to both	• Co-activating leader values are discovered to be in synch with younger generations but only when the distractions of communication differences and physical separation are taken away. When realized, both younger and older generations gain insight and respect for the others' social purviews
Leader Intent	• Co-activating leaders initially share vision and inspiration through face-to-face interactions and encourage other co-activating leaders to do the same spreading leader intent throughout informal networks	• Co-activating leaders create leverage opportunities through other co-activating leaders when they share vision, mission, and goal attainment resulting in shared language and context that is multiplied throughout the enterprise through indirect ties	• Co-activating leaders establish a common cultural value base by sharing personal experience and intent with other co-activating leaders who then in turn help others to understand how they are interdependent on many throughout the organization and have many ties through association
360 Degree Vision	• Co-activating leaders use influence to bridge physical distance gaps when needed through opening themselves to a complete view of all stakeholders	• Co-activating leaders reduce communication problems by understanding their target audience and using influence techniques that extend their vision up, down, and around	• Co-activating leaders work to saturate all levels of stakeholders with common values and respect for everyone in the stakeholder ecosystem helping all to feel more connected to those in other social circles

(continued)

105

TABLE 7.3 Reducing Virtual Distance through Co-Activating Leaders *(Continued)*

Co-Activating New Leaders	Reducing Virtual Distance Through Co-Activating Leaders		
	Physical Distance	Operational Distance	Affinity Distance
Adaptive Communication	• Co-activating leaders know when to be face-to-face with different stakeholder levels and adapt their communication style to get the most out of virtual and face-to-face meetings	• Co-activating leaders pay close attention to what level they are talking with and use different kinds of communications to ensure that their message is heard and internalized reducing the guesswork needed to understand context and increasing information sharing	• Co-activating leaders adapt to others' communication styles helping those in the organizational ecosystem to feel that they are similar in values systems to others and therefore more closely linked through shared goals and missions
Self-Activating Leaders	• Co-activating leaders encourage others to reach out and do what's needed, including meeting with others face-to-face, to make the most of their relationships	• Co-activating leaders make it clear that to minimize complexity in multi-dimensional work environments, other leaders need to take their own lead in providing the context and information others need to be successful	• Co-activating leaders establish the need for others to build their own social networks and widen their access to others in the organization which strengthens the entire group through "weak ties" with others.

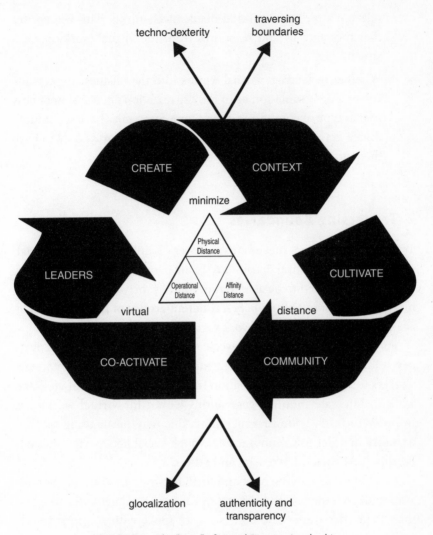

FIGURE 7.2 The "How" of Virtual Distance Leadership

human cues as possible is recommended. Using video-mail is an option when video-conferencing or face-to-face technologies are not available.

c. Does the message contain a lot of data that needs to be synthesized? If yes, use e-mail and other e-based options and include relevant attachments and feedback mechanisms. This will ensure that messages to and responses from the virtual workforce are streamlined.

d. Whether to leverage virtual worlds into the business process involves a determination as to the organization's cultural openness to that type of communication. Some companies have spent inordinate amounts of money developing virtual worlds only to have them go unused.

2. Traversing Boundaries

Traversing boundaries means crossing over disciplinary, organizational, geographic, and cultural divisions to bring people and groups together. Today's leaders need to be able to move fluidly, between different organizational zones, but also *amongst* different groups of people bound by age differences and social network variants.

For example, the notion of reverse mentoring is a way to co-activate new leaders. This means that leaders move, for instance, among younger workers to better digest information from a different point of view and work to integrate multiple generations within the virtual workforce. In order to reach younger generations this may mean using techno-dexterity in order to communicate through social networking sites like Facebook, MySpace, Linked-In, and others.

In addition to moving back and forth between generational boundaries, today's leaders need to also travel across social networks to maximize their effectiveness. Some leaders we spoke with continue to rely mainly on traditional social networks like professional associations. However many have added online social networking as well. Many authorities host their own blogs, inviting people from all walks of life to discuss common interests. This kind of open engagement fuels interest in the company and its mission.

The key to traversing boundaries is to summon up a kind of courage to face new situations that are hard to control and difficult to predict. This often flies in the face of what leaders normally like to do. Therefore a certain degree of tolerance for ambiguity of the social kind, as opposed to market forces more readily internalized by control-minded leaders, is required.

3. Glocalization

Since the early days of trade when people traveled thousands of miles to swap goods and services, the dynamic tension between global and local issues has been at work. But never before, by the push of a button, have we been able to act so globally while staying so local. Whether you're on a web conference with people from New York and Taiwan or sending e-mail across oceans, interactions with people all over the world happen all the time and the frequency of these interactions is increasing.

The recent rapid deterioration of financial markets across most modern countries is testament to the fact that we work in an intensely connected global network economy. We cannot ignore the health and well-being of our far-flung virtual neighbors. However, as human beings we deal with day-to-day life at the local level; going to the grocery store, filling our car with gasoline at the corner station, and taking our children to school just a few blocks away. So both global as well as local issues continuously need our attention.

More than ten years ago the term "think global, act local" led to the term *glocalization* in marketing. And that slogan has never had so much value as it has now. The leader's ability to take a balanced view of the workforce from both the global as well as local level is a different kind of glocalization that's critical for the Virtual Distance Leader to understand.

The workforce is glocalized. People live and work within the context of their local towns, cities, and countries. And yet they must somehow be ready, willing, and able to act on behalf of a worldwide mission. To motivate people to act in this way leaders need to use glocalized communications—sending messages and employing work practices that speak to both.

Our example from HP speaks to this issue well. Phil McKinney deploys a strategy whereby people on new product development teams are moved inside the local culture in which the product will ultimately be delivered. Once their assignment is finished, they return to their home country where information about global issues can be shared.

Glocalization requires leaders to have an outside-in perspective while working from the inside-out. Translation of issues to abstract and more global views is required at times. Translation of issues to specific local concerns is required at other times. Leaders need the skills and prowess to do both.

4. Authenticity and Transparency

In 2003 Bill George, the former CEO of Medtronics, published a book called *Authentic Leadership*.[2] In it he argues for a new kind of leader—one that would never accept the state of affairs brought on by Enron's failed head and others. And there's no doubt that authenticity still remains a key element in how a leader goes about communicating with followers and others that might be hovering in nearby virtual vicinities.

However, what is not emphasized is that authenticity must come through all modes of communication. It's one thing to exude genuineness when one is face to face alongside others. It's another thing to try and reflect that virtue through virtual channels. This takes practice, talent, and unrelenting commitment to oneself, as well as the virtual workforce. And transparency goes hand in hand with this notion of authenticity. Those in charge, with the power and the authority to lead, need not only be true to themselves and others but also willing to share information that may or may not be seen as favorable. As Bill George said,

> People are too well informed to adhere to a set of rules or to simply follow a leader over a distant hill.[3]

People are well informed but they also know that much is still hidden from them. It is this knowledge and the rampant reports of leaders gone bad that fuels a sense of pervasive distrust. To overcome this, leaders not only have to show they are authentic, they must also make public information that the informed virtual workforce needs to know—has to know—if they are to earn and keep their trust.

CONCLUSION

New leadership models are scarce. It's easy and comfortable to say that we need the same kinds of leader behaviors, personalities, and situational positioning in the virtual workforce as we do in the traditional workforce. And in part, that's true. This book is not meant to argue that traditional models are completely irrelevant. However, relying on old models alone, built using outdated assumptions that no longer apply, is getting us nowhere in terms of moving the virtual workforce ahead.

As described in Chapter 2, old leadership models can be categorized into three compartments: trait-based, contingency-based, and behavorial-based, as Figure 7.3 shows.

What's needed is to consider the virtual workforce as the context in which all leadership is brought forward. And to do this we must then also consider Virtual Distance—the most significant change to the dynamics of social behavior in the last 100 years. When we do so, we find that an action-based leadership model is called for and it's called the **Virtual Distance Leadership Model**. This model takes into account that leader styles vary; however, the actions leaders must take to maximize

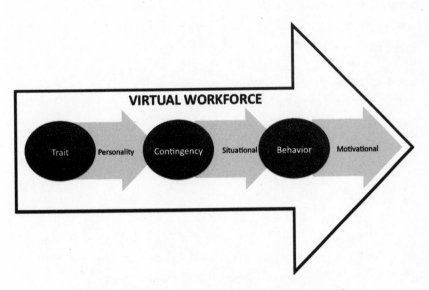

FIGURE 7.3   Traditional Leader Models and the Virtual Workforce

productivity and innovation in the globally integrated enterprise are quite clear. They must:

1. **Create context**
2. **Cultivate community**
3. **Co-activate new leadership**

through:

1. **Techno-dexterity**
2. **Traversing boundaries**
3. **Glocalization**
4. **Authenticity and transparency**

Taken together, these actions and the paths followed reduce Virtual Distance. We can no longer rely on ancient techniques to enhance social well-being in the virtual organization enough to change outcomes and advance agendas. The Virtual Distance Leader pulls people together across virtual landscapes, fostering a sense of hope, and a shared responsibility for creating a brighter and more solid foundation for the future.

NOTES

1. K. Sobel Lojeski, R. Reilly, *Uniting the Virtual Workforce: Transforming Leadership and Innovation in the Globally Integrated Enterprise* (Hoboken, NJ: John Wiley & Sons 2008).
2. W. George, *Authentic Leadership* (San Francisco: Jossey-Bass, 2003).
3. www.usnews.com/usnews/news/articles/061022/30authentic.htm

CHAPTER **8**

The Future of Leadership As We Know it

n this book many varied views of leadership have been shared from some of the world's best. Those profiled take certain actions to inspire, motivate, and manage in a way that's different than what they might have done just a few years ago. These actions better meet the fluid demands of the virtual workforce. As has been pointed out, the virtual workforce is a relatively new phenomenon; one that time-tested management models simply never accounted for. Business models designed at the turn of the twentieth century were done so in light of a dualistic mindset in which managers knew all and workers knew nothing. These power relationships were essential to building and maintaining control of the organization. They were the bedrock upon which bureaucracies were built. Leadership roles were clear, undeniable, and went unquestioned.

However, as we've moved past these kinds of leader-follower relationships at a time when information and communication technology has become central to the way we work, changing everything about how we communicate and relate to one another, yesterday's traditional "workers" have morphed into today's professionals. The current array of virtual workers is comprised of people with specialized skills and extensive education. They don't simply sink into submersed low-status bubbles blown from tired old views. And yet, none of our leadership models have been designed from the outset to address this new population of wired, always-on, highly informed individuals, until now.

Although the leaders interviewed clearly have an open view of the world, many others still live a life looking much like it did 50 years ago; traveling comfortably as needed, relying on downstream managers and other support to get things done, and feeling unencumbered by whatever lies beyond the office door. This results in decreasing empathy between the leader and the virtual workforce. And without much empathy coupled with rising Virtual Distance, leaders can become highly disconnected from the realities of their own corporate workforce. Leaders might and often do lose sight of what's important in the short term as well as in terms of developing the foundations needed for the long term, often doing little to assuage concern about the perception that leaders care little about the issues that don't concern them personally.

As stated before but worth repeating here, a mere 7 percent of Americans have any faith in today's leaders, while only 8 percent believe we're developing good leaders for the future. At the same time, just 10 percent of corporate leaders use new social media tools, even as the vast majority of virtual workers are actively engaged with one another through social networks.

Oddly, while their worldwide employees communicate freely with each other, many executives barricade themselves behind electronic doors, seeing little of the world in which their workforce lives. They perpetuate a self-centered safe haven that runs counter to the experiences of other corporate citizens. It's no wonder that views of leaders continue to slide. Much needs to be done.

The Virtual Distance Leadership Model begins with one simple assumption; everything about the way we work and interact with one another has changed at every level. Moving forward, this has implications for every leader charged with managing the virtual workforce. We can no longer assume for example that everyone can possibly know enough about others on their team to understand their meaning. Leaders need to create context in a way that motivates and inspires people to act on their behalf—people who are thousands of miles apart and potentially worlds away in terms of their worldview. Simply holding a position of authority and giving talks to large groups now and then is not enough.

The notion of community building has to be reawakened in the virtual realm. We no longer live and work with the same people. We live with our neighbors across the street but work with our neighbors across the ocean. Therefore communities don't naturally emerge in the confines of the work setting. And trying to mimic social phenomena like the viral spread of Facebook in the context of a corporate population doesn't work either.

People in organizations need to operate in a fashion that forwards organizational group goals. Relying on serendipity among unrelated individuals to spawn innovation in a completely unstructured fashion doesn't fly without some leadership and guidance. Corporate community building must take advantage of free-flowing web-based space but keep things moving in a direction that satisfies financial and competitive interests as well. And for this, leaders need to get actively involved in on-line as well as face-to-face community development.

Simply plopping in an instantiation of some virtual world and expecting people to join will not do either. There is no "field of dreams" for the virtual workforce. Building it does not mean they will come. More importantly, simply having the tools does not mean that people know how to talk to each other in a meaningful, respectful, and productive way especially when Virtual Distance is high. Leaders need to thoughtfully cultivate a sense of belonging to a greater connected good and do so over the virtual airwaves extending their presence over multiple modes of communication.

Building community means creating sustainable critical mass dispersed among thousands of collocated and distributed individuals all working in concert. In addition, leaders today need to loosen up their view of control. This is one of the most challenging endeavors of all. Most leaders believe they need to hold on to control in order to be effective. And while this in part, remains true, working with others to take on leadership roles is more important than ever and can't be done well unless a leader can let go of the tight grip they have on themselves and the illusion of control they think they have over others. Co-activating new leaders is essential to spreading mission and vision throughout informal social networks. And it is upon this lattice that things get done in the twenty-first century.

However we are a long way off from having substantial numbers of leaders take up this position. Take for example the accelerated spread of social networking tools such as Twitter. There isn't a news program around that doesn't offer the opportunity to post a "tweet." And many do. Yet corporate executives are generally too slow to move into this speedy and unconventional realm. As Ellen Pearlman, former Editor-in-Chief of *CIO Insight Magazine* and contributing editor for CIOZone.com reports,

> ... if a company thinks it is doing the right thing by tying its employees' hands because they want to control "the message" and don't trust them to blog without supervision, that company is living in the dark ages. If a company doesn't trust its employees or customers it's already in serious trouble.
>
> New research from The Conference Board indicates that only 1/3 of the executives studied regularly monitor social networking sites for information about their companies and only 10 percent participate in them. We've all got a lot to learn about new media and how best to use it for business advantage.[1]

However the leaders profiled in this book have jumped into the technological fray, actively taking part in twenty-first century communications while serving age-old human needs as well. They look for opportunities to get to know the younger generation, seek out ways to further leverage more experienced workers, and admittedly understand that the very nature of leadership itself is changing. During the course of our interviews we asked them to comment on how they would counsel others. Here are some of the responses:

> One thing I would say is if you come into new responsibilities to manage somebody who is not in your office and who is somewhere around the world, the first thing you have to do is get face-to-face with them. You have to start that way. And then from there you can taper off on how often you're face-to-face and continue to build a relationship. I have seen so many situations where the manager's been assigned new responsibilities but they don't take the time to go and meet their people. The relationship just doesn't ever really get off the ground. I believe you've got to have that human interaction at least once at the beginning.
>
> The other thing is that you've got to be clear, consistent, available. If you're going to schedule a one-on-one with a person every other week, don't cancel them. Be there for those people. They have to know that you're interested in what they're doing. And everybody wants to have an opportunity to say, look at what I'm doing. Look at my work. Give me your feedback. Is it what you want? Are we on the right track? That sort of thing. Don't shortchange them just because out of sight, out of mind thinking can take over.
>
> —Susan Roser, Senior Vice President, Global Service Support,
> Western Union

> Buckle your chin strap! I would say stop thinking like DOS and start thinking like LINUX. You know, we are in an open architecture world. Be porous, be willing to accept input and invite it and be willing to provide information in a much more asymmetrical, as needed, customized way. Be less formal. Be more inviting to the diversity of all the potential stakeholders whether they're your employees or your stockholders or your customers. And configure your day, your priorities in a way that invites that diversity. It creates lots of tension because it is not as pretty as a more controlled world that maybe we have experienced in the past, but it is incredibly rich in terms of how much you can learn and share and expose people to—not only to your point of view in terms of your organization, but you as a person. I think the biggest single risk in the twenty-first century is de-personalizing leadership. That the power of individual leaders will get lost in the technology. Indeed, you'll get de-sensitized to the impact of what it's like to feel leadership.

Patton made a point of getting out there with bullets whizzing around his head and standing on a tank with a silver helmet on and pearl-handled revolvers. That's a metaphor, but it's a fact that it's still important to make that personal leadership visible. Visibility is still critical even with all the messiness going on.

—Robert McMahon, President U.S. Commercial Operations,
Merck & Co., Inc.

Nurture creativity. It's the only way you're going to get the new solutions, the new innovative ideas, the new discoveries. And that's not a lecture, that's a culture. Truly understand the power of an emotionally compelling experience that people can have and if they can't have it find ways you can retell it for them in a very good story.

—Cheri Sterman, Director Child Development and
Consumer Relationships, Crayola

First of all be an open communicator. You can only be effective if you communicate openly about your plans, your goals, your strategy, and so on. Which means you empower people to take on a leadership role and execute so that not every time a decision has to be taken in the company, the decision needs to be escalated to those people that have the power to decide. Only when there is really an issue that needs to be solved and you can't find a solution, then of course, you have to escalate. And that is the reason why we have leaders and managers in the company.

Also, very important is strategy. It's not always the top that comes up with the strategy. It's an interaction of course between top management and what the base in your organization think, what they think should be the direction. Because sometimes we see that internal ventures that provide big wins for the company in terms of revenue and growth are not compliant with the strategy that has been set out which means that leaders in the company should also be open to re-discuss the strategy and refine it if they see that there are elements from the base that think opportunities are elsewhere than management thinks. So being open and discussing and refining the strategy and seeing that it is a bottom up as well as a top town approach is very important these days.

—Guido Petit, Director Alcatel-Lucent Technical Academy,
Alcatel-Lucent

Sometimes you just need to forget about your mission. Just hire the best people. There's a set of people who I know are just incredible and often I'll dip into that set even though I don't yet know where I'm going. If you hire the best people, they'll help you figure out the right direction.

I think it's also critical that you enjoy what you do, so you can be enthusiastic about it. There's nothing more infectious than an enthusiastic leader. You motivate people because you're being genuine. You've got to be excited about your own mission, your own vision, and do whatever you can to pave the way for your team to be successful. And you must network—networking is critical. You can't pave the way for your team and create a great environment if you're not out there networking with other people who can help you achieve your goals or help you take a different direction. Get out there yourself and let people see that you're a real person. Don't be too buttoned up, afraid to go travel and blog and interact in the community. There's huge value in the interpersonal, especially face-to-face opportunities

—Gina Poole, Vice President Software Group Marketing 2.0, IBM

One thing is to recognize the change we're facing today both throughout society and the world. Recognize that the value of the individual is not constrained by the person who is directly on your team but on the broader team that can influence your success. It's about an ecosystem of people not just people who are sitting within the 100 foot radius of you as a manager or as a leader.

I think also understand what people are looking for from leaders which is not the answer, but someone who can be the cheerleader, the encourager, the person who recognizes that it's not about giving the definitive answer but in creating the environment that allows people to bring their creativity to the table to solve real issues, real problems that have impact in building products and capabilities and services. I guess I get frustrated with leaders who think they've got to have the definitive final answer and that everybody needs to be in a line and march versus asking themselves how do you engage the heart and passion of your people. Irrespective of whether you're an Obama fan or not you can't deny Obama's ability to get people to bring to the table their heart and passion for a cause. And for leaders today, it's about how do you engage the heart and passion of your people for a cause. Rather than thinking of your resources and people

as a cog in the wheel. And managers who understand how to unleash the passion of their people are the ones that I think will be successful.
—Phil McKinney, Vice President and CTO, Personal Systems Group,
Hewlett Packard Company

The digital age has shifted the balance of power. Compensation has also shifted from people being paid for longevity, to now being paid for contribution to the organization. People are valued not necessarily because they have an ancient history with the organization but more if they can be able to operate in the current mode. So you can't hold yourself up on a pedestal and think that you don't have to learn new things.
—Kathy Burke-Thomas, Associate Director,
AT&T Project Management Center of Excellence, AT&T

Technology can bring insight, information, and understanding through better data mining, but at times there is conflicting data, competing missions and you've got to decide one way or the other. Technology on the whole can be a distracter from the decision you need to make. The only thing I have drawn from this, is that I should never make a really important decision without sleeping on it.
—Lawrence A. McAndrews, CEO, National Association of
Children's Hospitals and Related Institutions (NACHRI)

It's about being positive, it's about being encouraging, it's about empowering your people and enabling them to be the best they can be; it's about directing, not managing and it's about communication. These are the most important things you have to pay attention to. And then, of course, being empathetic. Especially in an executive technology role because the technology touches everything in this corporation so I have to deal with everybody and so I had better have some kind of understanding of what drives them as a corporate officer, as a corporate manager, as a corporate individual contributor, what drives people personally. Especially if it's one on one, or one on not too many, communication has a lot to do with empathy. And be aware that not everybody, not all the people around you are all like you. Do not manage from the inside out but instead manage from the outside in.

From the inside out is thinking first about you and then making the leap to thinking everybody likes what I like. Everybody should be interested in this. Everybody should behave that way because I behave that

way. From the outside in is taking the information and understanding there is a whole spectrum of thoughts, ideas, behaviors out there that you may have to deal with and they're all different. They're not necessarily like yours and so keep an open mind.
—Jack Barsky, Vice President of Information Technology, NRG

CONCLUSION

It is important to keep in mind that this book was not written to argue for some panacea-like alternative where technology is dismantled in favor of a world in which people only work with people face-to-face, never picking up a communication device. In fact, throughout history many different types of communication technologies have been used including cave paintings from the earliest days of man all the way up and including information and communication technology. However, it is safe to say that until the advent of intelligent devices carrying messages immediately accessible to all who use them, there has never been such a deluge of exchanges that lack the requisite context to interpret appropriate meaning. And it is this characteristic that we need to consider closely against the backdrop of technological capabilities that allow us to work together across continents, cultures, and varying organizational constructs.

What we do see is an ever-growing and urgent need for extensive and fundamental re-thinking about the way leaders interact with the people who work for them either directly or indirectly—the human beings that are the virtual workforce. Under a barrage of incoming e-mail and unending lists of to-dos the virtual workforce needs leaders who engage them in a way that makes their life at work more meaningful; leaders who are willing to modify organizational models to accommodate new realities.

In summary, while many acknowledge that the world is a very different place, especially in the area of technology-enabled communications, little effort has been made to really examine and rework leadership models to meet new needs. Around the world there are growing concerns about the effectiveness of corporate leaders. Skeptical views of future success are driven in part by the chasms that lie between the hardened management models we rely upon and the reality that none of them use assumptions that look anything like the actual circumstances in which the virtual workforce exists. Keeping this in mind, leaders of today's organizations can follow the lead of those profiled in this book. With just a few adjustments, our readers can begin to crack open the shells they are surrounded by and see a better way forward.

NOTE

1. www.ciozone.com/index.php/Management/Twitter-and-All-That-Jazz/Six-Rules-for-using-the-Web-to-Create-a-Rave.html

CHAPTER 9

A Different View of Leadership Altogether

I n this book some light has been shed on how great leaders do things differently to inspire and motivate the virtual workforce. But how do great leaders get inspired themselves? In 1954 Albert Einstein wrote the following:

> A human being is part of the whole called by us universe, a part limited in time and space. We experience ourselves, our thoughts and feelings as something separate from the rest. A kind of optical delusion of consciousness. This delusion is a kind of prison for us, restricting us to our personal desires and to affection for a few persons nearest to us. Our task must be to free ourselves from the prison by widening our circle of compassion to embrace all living creatures and the whole of nature in its beauty. The true value of a human being is determined by the measure and the sense in which they have obtained liberation from the self. We shall require a substantially new manner of thinking if humanity is to survive.[1]

So how fitting it was that the interview with Steven Tainer, a scholar of contemplative traditions, was at the time visiting Prof. Piet Hut at the Institute for Advance Study in Princeton, New Jersey. This was Albert Einstein's workplace for over 20 years! Steven is too young to have known Einstein, but I suspect they would have agreed on a lot of things. Like Einstein, Steven Tainer is about as far removed from corporate life as one can be. Where Einstein was a man of science who had an interest in spirituality and philosophy, Steven is a man of spirituality and philosophy who has a strong interest in science (he was a philosopher of science earlier in life). Together with his colleague Piet Hut and some other scientists and scholars, he founded the Kira Institute; an organization devoted to promoting mutual understanding between science and contemplative disciplines. Steven has spent forty years studying, teaching, and writing about Eastern philosophy and contemplative practice. It may seem strange to include an interview with an expert on contemplation in traditions like Buddhism and Taoism, but I felt so strongly that Steven's ideas were important for today's leaders that his interview is included here.

> **Lojeski:** In this book, I look at various business leaders and get their input on leadership in this new global community of ours. You, of course, aren't involved in business but I'm very interested in your concept of what leadership is. Do you think of leadership in the way that most people think of leadership or do you think of it in some other way?

> **Tainer:** Well, obviously there are a lot of different notions regarding what a leader is. But I want to find natural processes for helping people mature and become themselves more truly, so I look to natural relationships that differ from the typical leadership angle. Parent-child and family relationships are good examples, as is friendship—a wonderful model. Similarly, the exemplar relationship is a good kind of model. If somebody has found himself or herself in a true and fundamental way, then he or she can live in an exemplary way for other people. That's influential not because you're overtly trying to influence people, but because they recognize intuitively something

of what you've become. And then they draw their own conclusions about its relevance for their own situation.

There are probably other natural relationships that are worth tapping for cues or clues. The one that I avoid is the stereotypical notion of a leader, because it often involves a charismatic person or personality who then influences (in a worrisome sense of the word) other personalities to follow. That to me is just borderline evil. Perhaps it too is "natural," but in a quite different sense. Historically, it seems to have produced much trouble for human beings, not the least of which is that people may end up living out a whole life without ever finding themselves. Instead, they just end up being "influenced." If I'm going to influence someone, it's by encouraging them to be enthusiastic about life and to find themselves. And I try to suggest specific docking maneuvers and point out resources in their own nature that help them zero in. But beyond that, no.

There's a real being present who can be uncovered and brought out more explicitly. There's also a circumstantially-defined being that is not fully representative of the real person. If I can help people distinguish between those two things, and then tap into their own basic living resources, plus their unique individual resources, and help these latter all come out more, then I'm happy.

So in conclusion, I think the typical leadership notion is one that we are better off without. Do you have a comment about that? This is all a preface to your real question, which was about serenity and contemplation.

Lojeski: I am also unhappy with traditional leadership models. One issue that concerns me is the falling level of trust in leaders today. Can you talk about trust as an element of the people you work with? When they begin to see the real self or the true self does that make a difference?

Tainer: An ordinary sense of personality, an ordinary sense of oneself—what I typically call a kind of self-image—is plagued by doubt. That sense of oneself has lots of trust issues, because it's always disconnected from other things in life. But if you discover more of what you are in various natural senses, then you also find that you're not an isolate among isolates. And once someone has a sense of herself as being fundamentally part of the world, life, other people, basic values and ethical responses etc., then trust becomes a different kind of thing, one that's very natural and easy because it's guided by grounded insight.

People need to give themselves a chance to find, express and enact what they feel. But often, the other voice keeps jumping in and says "how do you know that, how can you be sure, why do you think that? What about all these things I want"—that the self image wants—"why aren't you trying to further those as well?" There are a lot of internal dialogues that play out along these lines, but as someone learns that the self-image is really limited and even unhelpful, and they become more comfortable excavating and trusting the other part, then truly grounded trust becomes increasingly available. You see, you know. For instance, "this person is somebody I have a connection to," "this person needs help," "this person is suffering." You see things directly. And if you don't, you admit that and act accordingly. No wobble.

Lojeski: Do people have a duality? When you work with them do they shift back and forth between these two? What happens in the process?

Tainer: Human beings are improbable creatures. What other creature on the planet takes forty years to grow up? I mean seriously, it's almost an impossible notion! You just wouldn't expect that such a thing could exist in a biologically-framed universe. But we do in fact need that much time, and I don't think there is a shortcut. So the process is messy. Along the way, it involves lots of strange tangents and gaps or falling back, for various reasons. We need to accept and be patient with this natural pattern of maturation, while recognizing that it does need some guidance.

I understand that in certain scientific contexts, my way of talking might be misunderstood, but I'm trying to push the realization that there is such a thing as a nature that we have, or various types of natures, in fact. A living nature is one thing that we all share in common.

The kind of individual unique nature that we have (as a particular person) is another one. The fundamental human kind of nature is yet a third. Each of us is a human being and we need to grow up into that and actively be a real human being on an ongoing basis, rather than just passively assuming that our *homo sapiens* biological heritage does the job. The latter doesn't guarantee that we've lived up to being a human being or that we're *fully* enacting our humanity.

Leading tends to imply impressing someone, so that they then want to be like the leader, and that's exactly what I'm saying shouldn't happen. I think people should want to be like themselves, more truly themselves. In a sense that's harder. It's actually quite easy to say "you should be like me" etc. "I have money, you want money. Follow me, you'll have money, you'll have sex, you'll have fame, you'll have acceptance into society" and so on. That's easy because the mechanisms in the human being that you appeal to get that stuff going are child-level ones, very simplistic and coercive. They're very effective button pushers, but poor guides.

There's no button you push to get someone to mature into themselves. By its very nature, this is more difficult to achieve than the simplistic leadership emphasis, which just bypasses all the real maturation issues.

People find serenity and peace, and reacquire a grounded sense of self, by coming back to what they really are. The more you can perceive this in yourself on the aliveness level, which is one simple place you can start, the more you can find that you have a living nature which can be disrespected only with serious consequences. You can feel those consequences very quickly. It's useful feedback, and guides you to live better.

As an experiment, you can try certain things that go against the grain, and then see how trashed you feel and how that affects your day and your perception of life, the world, happiness, and connection to others. The usual way we live is tainted by disrespect for our living nature, our unawareness of it. So just by helping people find that aliveness in themselves and then helping them see what happens when they respect it (or don't), they can then immediately clue into that more, and can rest in it more.

If you take someone at random and say "relax now!," what they will usually think it means is that they should adopt a pose of stillness and try to have fewer thoughts, or that they should have a particular "relaxed" sensation. But what would it really mean to be relaxed? We have the ordinary word "relax." And everyone knows it, and thinks they also know what it means in practice. But I'm pretty sure there are not a thousand people in the United States who can truly relax.

It's not just about being "loose or lax," but letting go of extraneous stuff, coming back to yourself in some authentic way and abiding within that . . . living from that. And if you don't have any idea of what's extraneous, or of what is there to come back to, or how to abide within it, then relaxation can never be much more than a somewhat frustrating attempt at an elusive goal. Most people confuse it with being tranquilized or something. You just take a pill and go out for a while. But that's not being relaxed. And like being "led," it's not a basis for living well.

The same point applies to these other aspects of our nature that should be elicited by encouragement, example, and a proper maturation process. People can relax, find peace, regain their ground by just coming back to what they are fundamentally, to the extent that they have identified that and learned how to emphasize it. If it comes to mean anything else, then it's just as you suggested: People slip back and forth, forever, rather than just temporarily, as part of a focused process of learning and growing into themselves. They'll have very little notion of serenity, contentment, poise.

The word "contentment" means the same thing more or less as the word "containment." Etymologically they're about the same word. The whole point of being contained is that you stay within what you are. You don't keep leaving that and stepping instead into this self-image, which is what people normally live as—that's slipping around, "leaving" and getting lost.

Lojeski: The real self. Is there a distinction between the real self and the ego? In other words, I perceive myself as being apart from the rest of the world. I exist and I am different from the rest of the world and then you talk about the sense of self. Are those two different things? Is the self a concept that is even valid?

Tainer: The issue is simply a human one of understanding through your own direct experience that you can be inauthentic or untrue to yourself. You can acquire so many secondary or imported character- istics that you've just sort of lost something precious. And you can also go the other direction. This is an empirical observation.

I sometimes tell my students to find three movies that are on the same subject, like three James Bond movies, or three Jane Austen films, whatever, with a similar kind of central character. Just watch them back-to-back. Spend a day watching those movies. And then see who you think you are. And see what you think the world is. Human beings are very suggestible—our cognitive equipment includes the capacity to rapidly take on new sense of self and new sense of context.

We acquire these secondary senses of self extremely readily. That's how, as infants and children, we can begin to set ourselves up. And that's what we're always doing. In that process, we're effectively saying: "this is where I am now. This is what can happen to me in this world." So if you go see three scary movies, for instance, it's going to definitely affect your sense of what's likely to happen to you. It's not an acquired hypothesis in the formal sense, but more a complex reaction formed by suggestibility. So that's an example of how you take on false or limited senses of self (as well as useful or relevant ones).

Anyway, in little experiments like this, you can actually watch yourself become reframed, and then gradually recover again. So, *to what* are you recovering? As you gradually emerge from all these acquired images, you can actually observe the process. Is there a hard and fast, totally clear line of demarcation between the one kind of acquired sense of self and the other? No, I'm not claiming that, at least not for most of us as we make our way through the many circumstances and influences of our busy lives. But we can still make some important distinctions quite empirically and concretely, and benefit by doing so.

So what I am emphasizing is the difference between simply passively acquiring traces from circumstances and then saying "that's who I am," versus maturing into something demonstrably more true to ourselves, more satisfying. In the former case, we inherit all the mental patterns, emotions and perspectives that go with the traces ... it's a whole constellation of "self" fragments, unconsciously-acquired and perpetuated by habit, just habit. But in the other case, while there's still a sense of self that draws from one's past and current circumstances and so on, it does so in order to truly learn. The circumstances are then seen as part of a kind of living context which brings the real being out. We can both discover and author ourselves, rather than just being "written" by events or influences.

A tradition like Buddhism, which I teach, talks about "not-self," but this doesn't contradict what I'm saying here. I'll just mention that point in passing—it would take more time than we have to discuss it properly here.

Lojeski: Can you talk about the notion of happiness as a construct and whether that interferes with finding the true self or not?

Tainer: "Happiness" is derived from an ancient word "happ" which literally means circumstances and luck. So most of what people call happiness just involves becoming addicted to circumstances working out a certain way that the more superficial sense of self likes. So people hope to be lucky and are "happy" when they are. They hope to have the circumstances that the little self, the selfish self, wants and they don't want anything else to happen because if it did they would be unhappy. So the ordinary notion of happiness is often tied to being lucky with circumstances, based on whatever a person's passively-acquired preferences might be. And avoiding being "unlucky," of course.

But for me happiness would better be understood as a natural response to coming back to yourself, then working and appreciating life as an opportunity to step even more into that real being and the being's full context, which includes other people, the whole society and so on. Happiness then ceases to mean simply luck with circumstances, pandering to narrow preferences, but being true to your nature and to your real context. We recognize responsibilities pertaining to being a true part of that world, and find happiness in the discovery. We even recognize something as being a "right action," we see it spontaneously and can trust our perception.

Lojeski: So ethical behavior comes from that and it comes from that naturally?

Tainer: Absolutely. I think it can't come from any other place. Appeal to convention or dogma, or providing narrowly rational or logical arguments for an ethical dimension won't suffice. You can only *find*—recognize—the ethical dimension and live in it. You cannot prove that there is such a thing to someone who doesn't want to live in it, or thinks of it as merely a "belief" to be acquired or debated. Those approaches won't work. You cannot "prove" ethics.

On the other hand, part of what I'm talking about actually requires healthy skepticism as part of the process of finding and testing mature ethical perception. So I'm not recommending being credulous or attaching to warm and fuzzy orientations because they feel good to you. The first thing you would have to do in contemplative training is say, "it feels good to whom? What sense of self? According to what kind of mind and what habits of mind and judgment?" That's what contemplation is all about. In learning to see what we've been led to believe or feel, what acquired habits we're using, we can see what we've been "sold." So skepticism as a tool is part of contemplation, but it's not negative or nihilistic skepticism. Eventually you find what you judge to be a good reason for trusting, for valuing certain things, for going one way rather than another and for being happy.

Lojeski: Is that skepticism always a part of your life or do you reach a point where you've gotten past skepticism?

Tainer: You eventually find higher kinds of mind at various levels, that are no longer merely skeptical, not because they've found something that's so sacred it can't ("shouldn't") be doubted, but because you see directly, as a higher analog to skepticism. It doesn't look like ordinary skepticism but is far more sagacious and critical than skepticism would ever be. The problem with the ordinary skeptical mind is that it can never take itself into account very well. What it tends to do is look outward, at an idea or perspective, and say "why should I trust that?" But in what I'm talking about, you have a mind that knows, in a way that is also very incisive, and isn't credulous or unclear about its own disposition or biases. It finds its own proper ground, and knows when that is lost . . . this is the way contemplative traditions see the issue.

This is related to the ethical stance that we were talking about. It's an aspect of that. You simply know, and act. If somebody leaves some mess on the floor here in the office, the ordinary self could say, "well it's not my mess, I have no obligation here." And then it would walk away. In what I'm emphasizing, the person would immediately know "Oh, a mess on the floor, I'm here with it, I'll clean it up *now*." Very straightforward. The same applies to higher-level ethical concerns too. We're talking about learning to care.

Lojeski: In what ways do you think technology plays a role in our lives today?

Tainer: You know we're all using computers and technology but what else are we doing? Maybe the answer is, not much. When I wrote a little monograph in 1997, of course, the technology was very different then. Things like the Internet and visual media have changed a lot, but even at that earlier point the statistic I read and quoted, was that people in the United States were already spending more time on a daily basis viewing mediated realities than in having a direct relationship with something; in terms of television-watching time, watching computer monitors and related media such as video games, etc. If you add it all up, the average person in some age groups is spending more time with visual media than with direct encounters—like having a cup of tea with a friend or family member. So while technology by itself can't necessarily be claimed to be undermining the maturation or grounding process that I'm recommending, it does seem to be what we're really engaged with most. That has consequences, and implicitly constitutes a dubious value judgment.

There's no balance to that picture. We're simply not spending enough time in a way that's committed to having a more appreciative engagement in life. It's becoming the ultimate bad scenario, where we have a precious thing that's being eroded away by influences which have that potential (among more positive ones) particularly because we don't even see what's being lost or how. We simply don't even know anymore that this "precious" aspect of life exists. We have no name for it; we have no common discussion about it that acknowledges it. Nothing in the society nurtures it. This brings us back to the leadership issue you're talking about, and what I think might properly replace leadership as ordinarily understood.

There's simply nothing in the contemporary picture that says you've got this precious dimension and you need to protect it and exercise it. I think the modern context is much more dangerous than the ancient world was, simply because it *can be*—there's the potential for going further off. But, by itself, technology is a great thing. My Tibetan teachers went totally gaga over media technology when they came to the West. I could see their eyes getting big when they learned about computers, and later about the internet—they were thinking "what we could do with *that?!*" But their idea was, "we could put all of our texts on that, we could send them around to everyone, we could meet together using that and encourage people to study or to do some kind of practice together or serve the community better."

They weren't thinking we could spend all of our time being totally alone, immersed in some kind of ridiculous secondary or tertiary thrall, marked by loss of presence. One of them called the latter scenario, which is so common now, a kind of "double delusion," where the tendencies all human beings have always had to be influenced in pernicious ways are exacerbated by the new media. The same point, pro and con, applies more generally to all technology, I suppose.

Technology is actually part of humanity's growing up process, part of the very maturation process that I was describing. But we as a species have entered into a funny teenage stage developmentally now, and that has extra dangers, as always with teenagers. The potential to get lost is definitely greater now than it was before.

To take a simple example, until the last century or so, human beings had a lot of downtime. We don't realize this anymore. There were big areas of Europe, for instance, that were pretty much asleep for the whole of winter, up through the 18th century. A person could go out into the countryside and not see anyone, because the people were all asleep most of the time. Maybe it was just too cold and that's all . . . I'll leave scholars and scientists to decide. But I do think perhaps there is more to the story. Human beings aren't really built to be running around frantically on the kinds of schedule that we find common now. It's possible to adapt, of course, and we humans do have a lot of plasticity too. But the current pattern may still not be "natural." Certainly I think we're currently just being lost . . . trashed by our schedules. It's a simple problem, you might think, but in practice it's one of the most difficult to solve.

There's no theoretical issue here; it's just that we're too busy, particularly with secondary things. The whole notion of "not doing too much" is so stigmatized now that few people see a positive value in just settling down a bit. You're only viewed as important, successful, if you're too busy. I know very few people who are comfortable when I say something like: "no, I don't think I'm going to do anything today," or "I haven't been doing much for the last several days." If I talk like that, they think, "he's lost it" or "he's not living up to his potential." It takes quite a lot of training—or deprogramming (!)—for people to see this in another light. And that's a problem too. It's just a cultural attitude, shaped partly by technological innovations in the workplace and at home.

Lojeski: If you look at the kind of society that the Tibetan Monks came from, for example, that society was not one that was concerned with people accumulating wealth.

Tainer: Tibet was one of the last examples in the world—now already gone of course—of a society where people really lived without a developed monetary system. They had only a few classes of people in the whole society. Yak herder types, nomadic people, and traders going in and out of the country on small jaunts, and gem merchants who could go further afield bringing things in from India and so on. There were also aristocrats, and a kind of monarchy formed from within the aristocracy. But most folks didn't have anything that you would call money. They just wanted very basic things like food and shelter, grazing land for livestock if they lived at the right altitude, etc. They didn't have a big food production system. Really, it was like a Bronze Age culture. And obviously I am hoping that we don't have to collapse back to a Bronze Age culture in order to see and value the things I am talking about.

I really meant it when I said that all of these new-fangled things like technology could be part of our maturation process. I think that the modern situation and what people are facing now is a great opportunity for better self-understanding. I don't think it's a big obstacle that we have to get around, just something human beings need to come to terms with, in order to continue to develop beyond even what they were able to realize in the past, as true human beings.

In a sense, I see the present situation as a proving ground or a training ground. This will play out for millennia probably. It may be hundreds of thousands of years before we fully understand what a human being is. So I am very positive about the present. I am just more sober than I used to be about how challenging it is. But yes, there is a tremendous opportunity now regarding learning what is really important, what contributes to that and what new questions can be asked that the ancients never even thought of. Certainly none of my teachers claimed that their traditions had "written the book" on human maturation and its final face. They were just saying, "This has been found to be a good direction to go in."

Lojeski: What's interesting is you talked about people doing nothing and they used to do this and still do in some cultures. But, the original notion of wealth and happiness was that you would get to a point where you could do nothing but instead we've gotten to a point where we have to keep working harder than ever and we never see that time to do nothing. In Moore's utopia you worked four hours a day and then had time to do whatever you wanted but as we've gotten more wealthy as a society we have less down time than ever.

Tainer: Yeah, and we use it being *busy!* If you take people in the modern culture and say "ok go on a vacation now or take some time off" what do people do? The answer is they find yet more ways of becoming stimulated, arguably over-stimulated, by media or activities of various sorts. The idea of really resting in some sense, relaxing with their spouse or playing with the kids, or just sitting together with friends, is not what's done.

So this insane level of activity is a problem, but even it too could be an opportunity. After I'd studied with my first Tibetan teacher and some other teachers for about eleven years, I took time off and deliberately got the most stressful job I could find in Silicon Valley. As part of the plan, I joined a start-up company doing very intensive work on computer graphics tech, the first company to do computer animation on home computers. My whole idea was that I would do this for seven years. Just throw myself into it . . . live the way other people do in the modern world. I wanted to see if the contemplative stuff I had been learning could be held in the midst of that kind of helter-skelter environment. I was working seven days a week, every day of the year, no holidays, no vacation time—a couple days of sick time in eight years, as it turned out to be.

And I found that I actually started to learn more about what my teachers had told me. Previous to this period, I had only vaguely understood what they were really saying. In the new situation, there were all kinds of things happening—the pressures, challenges, the distress, definitely the false "leadership" models, with the superficial senses of self, and the consequences etc. It was all very relevant to what I'd been taught earlier, even though the cultural setting was vastly different.

Out of this experiment, I saw better how important it is to find one's ground. And to share life from that ground. This is quite important even from a business perspective! A subject for another discussion sometime, perhaps. So I hope we can learn again how to enjoy being with each other . . . how to do it, and why—what sort of value is present in that situation? We also need to learn more about the forces that pull us away from recognizing and enjoying that value. At present, we only vaguely know, and are too numb to care. We don't know how to contend with the background influences and frenzy, and the intensification of these factors by new media.

Lojeski: Is there something you can tell readers about how to slow down, how to find some contemplative space in a healthy way in the context of today's situations?

Tainer: Well there are always several different sides to this. One side is to make an experiment of things that usually happen anyway in ordinary life. People go through life in a rather habit-ridden and hapless way that doesn't allow them to learn. But they can have the same life that they have already and simply add, "I'm going to learn from what I'm already doing." So if they just did some of the usual things, and then just built into their schedule a chance to reflect—"this is what I did and this is how I felt afterwards"—that would already be a great start.

The problem we have now is that people may live 83 years or whatever, but they don't learn 83 years of stuff. They learn 16 months worth, scattered over a much longer time, and then just repeat the patterns over and over again. So first of all I would say "don't necessarily change your life, but do at least learn what it's telling you." Perform actions and notice their consequences. I hope people can get better at noticing both what they're doing—how they're living—and what the results are.

If, for instance, I am getting tired, I will notice it about 20 minutes earlier than the average American does now. Or maybe 20 years earlier! Seriously, people just don't notice anymore. That's a tremendous problem. So if you are prone to getting sick in a certain way, you could learn from that because there's a lead-up and an onset which can be studied. There are tiny but important things that you could notice so much more quickly, if you put an experimental boundary around the situation. Gradually you could walk things back to the point where you could say, "this is where it started."

And, similarly, if you get angry or cranky at someone or something similar in your interpersonal relationships, why not learn from that rather than just saying, "it keeps happening to me, tell me what to do." There's the leadership trap again . . . I don't think people need to be told what to do, they just need to notice what they are doing. It's not like people can't learn. It just doesn't occur to them that that's where they should start.

Again: We've lost sight of our basic "living being" and human levels to such an extent that if we try to make a list of things we'd like to do, we seldom put anything on the list that really serves us well. Why don't we serve what we actually are, and do the same for each other too?

I've had students who felt life was hopeless, meaningless, valueless, that they were unloved. And after asking them a bunch of questions, I'd learn that they were sleeping five hours or less. So I would just say, "well what about eight hours?" and he or she would reply, "well, what good would that do? I'd be more rested, but so what? It wouldn't really change anything." An incredible perspective, really. But with some persistent encouragement, they would reluctantly spend a month getting eight hours of sleep. To their amazement, it made a vastly greater difference than they expected, in many ways.

Of course, what I usually teach involves much more concerted contemplative explorations on more subtle levels . . . I know it must seem that I am really big on rest and sleep, based on this interview! But anyway, even a simple experiment like this can yield some useful insights and benefits. What I'm really big on is *learning!*

Perhaps making a simple "adequate sleep" commitment for a whole month is already beyond what this book can successfully encourage its readers to undertake . . . but might they be nudged into trying it for just three days, no excuses? Then at the end of the experiment, they could ask themselves how the world, or at least their immediate context, looks. How does their sense of self look? Has it changed? How do relationships with other people look? What, specifically, do they see in the faces of other people? How do they feel, and how do they treat people, as a result? What would they like to do with their lives? What forces tend to push them towards lapses (disconnects), and with what consequences? What new decisions would they like to make, and how well do they follow through?

Anyone can perform that sort of experiment. And it's useful to try, because we're both living beings and beings of a certain sort—human beings, with human needs and capacities that need to be learned about, served and exercised, freed from influences that we can see actually lead us away from what we are in the truest sense.

It's this great opportunity in the basic human situation that I want to help people understand better and enjoy.

SOME FINAL THOUGHTS

Although Steven began the interview by discounting any notion that he could provide any useful information on leadership, his perspective and thoughts provided several insights important for leaders to understand.

First, those who find themselves in leadership positions can take steps to increase their self-awareness. There are many routes to self-awareness: 360 feedback, psychological testing, executive coaching, are a few of the popular methods used to provide insight into one's own behavior. Steven offers another approach—one that is much more powerful in the long run. The nice feature of this approach is that it can be done by anyone with a bit of planning and discipline. As Steven says, the goal is to understand who you really are as compared with what he calls the "circumstantially defined self." As he says, you don't have to be told what to do, you just have to notice what you do. Once we understand ourselves and our own behavior we can begin to understand how our behavior affects others.

A second insight is the connection between your true self, ethical behavior, and trust. As Steven points out, as we come to understand truly who we are we become more ethical and more trusting. Here is another case where Steven's insight squares with other research. The studies show that one of the most important characteristics of trustworthy people is integrity. The research also shows that trustworthy people not only inspire more trust on the part of others but are also more trusting of others. As we become more authentic we become more trustworthy and trusting. As a leader in a world where we seldom or sometimes never see our employees face-to-face, trust is essential.

Finally, Steven offers an experimental approach to life that provides a way of understanding the difference between the self and the context that surrounds the self. As we have discussed throughout these chapters, understanding context and how to create it is a key to leading in a virtual world.

NOTE

1. A. Calipari, F. Dyson, *The New Quotable Einstein* (Princeton, NJ: Princeton University Press, 2005) p. 206.

The Virtual Distance Model*

Virtual Distance is a concept that is threaded throughout our discussion of leadership. We first conceived the idea several years ago when we began to examine the problems that virtual teams were having. As we studied these teams it became clear that a kind of psychological distance was being created by a combination of factors that distributed teams typically encounter. In order to better understand our leadership model a brief discussion of Virtual Distance may be helpful.

FIGURE A.1   The Virtual Distance Formula

$$\text{Virtual} \atop \text{Distance} = \text{Physical} \atop \text{Distance} + \text{Operational} \atop \text{Distance} + \text{Affinity} \atop \text{Distance}$$

---

*This material was adapted from: K. Sobel Lojeski, R. Reilly, *Uniting the Virtual Workforce: Transforming Leadership and Innovation in the Globally Integrated Enterprise* (Hoboken, NJ: John Wiley & Sons, 2008).

The Virtual Distance Model contains three major dimensions:

1. *Physical distance*—those factors that are based on real location differences in both space and time

2. *Operational distance*—psychological gaps that grow due to the many day-to-day problems that arise in the workplace

3. *Affinity distance*—the emotional disconnects between virtual team members rooted in a lack of fundamental relationship development

Figure A.1 shows the formula for Virtual Distance.

PHYSICAL DISTANCE

Physical distance (see Figure A.2) represents the varied ways in which we're separated by real things including geography, time zones, and organizational affiliation. Globalization has dramatically altered the extent to which these kinds of distances exist between co-workers.

There are three components of physical distance included in the Virtual Distance Model:

1. Geographic distance

2. Temporal distance

3. Organizational distance

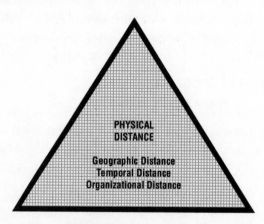

FIGURE A.2 Physical Distance

Geographic Distance

Geographic distance is simply what it says—the distances between us that can be measured using inches, feet, miles, and so on. Geographic distance is the factor which gets the most attention among managers and virtual team leaders. But it turns out that geographic distance is neither necessary nor sufficient to create Virtual Distance. But when it is an issue, it's a "fixed" condition, challenging us in many important ways, including finding methods that help us develop and maintain effective communications. Geographic distance contributes to a sense of being far away because, in fact, one *is* far away. So we cannot expect that people will be able to work through communication problems the way they would if they were face-to-face. And in today's modern workplace, it's often impossible or even undesirable to get together some, if not most, of the time.

Temporal Distance

Temporal distance is the separation caused by time zone differences as well as disparities in work schedules. The most significant issue that arises from time-related problems is coordinating work. Getting tasks into the right sequence and developing a steady rhythm among virtual team members is important to producing high-quality performance. But temporal distance wreaks havoc with this effort. Temporal distance specifically contributes to the sense that we're not well coordinated and can't establish any kind of predictable or regular rhythm.

Organizational Distance

Organizational distance is a sense of separateness brought on by differences in organizational affiliations. For example, Joe and Ramesh need to work together. Joe works for Acme Consumer Goods and Ramesh works for ABC Outsourcing. At a major chemical company, Jack and Jill are also required to work together. But Jill works in New Product Development and Jack works for the Supply Chain Management Division. Sometimes Jack and Jill need to talk to Joe and Ramesh because they're all involved in joint projects. Joe, Ramesh, Jack and Jill are organizationally distant from one another in varying degrees and these affiliation gaps fuel higher Virtual Distance. Organizational distance creates an impression of space because of differences in formal associations. We find people feeling as though they're not part of the same team even though they're assigned to work together toward the same ultimate goal.

Summary—Physical Distance

Physical distance creates the sense that others are far away because, for the most part, they really are. But as we discussed, Virtual Distance can be present in just as high levels when there isn't any physical distance whatsoever. The other two parts of Virtual Distance, operational and affinity distance, can play an even greater role in lowering performance among the twenty-first century virtual workforce.

OPERATIONAL DISTANCE

Operational distance (see Figure A.3) manifests as a sense that you're on a different playing field than those you work with each and every day. For example, have you ever had a "conference call from hell" when, after it was over, you wondered if you lived on the same planet as the people on the other end? If so, then you were experiencing operational distance—the impression that there's no connection between you and your counterparts. Day-to-day communication problems, task

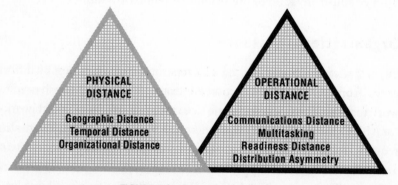

FIGURE A.3 Operational Distance

overloads, technology snags like crashing hard drives, and the dispersion of group members all pose major challenges and cause Virtual Distance to rise.

To understand how operational distance arises, we need to take a closer look at four key issues:

1. Communications distance
2. Multitasking
3. Readiness distance
4. Distribution asymmetry

Communications Distance

Communications distance often shows up as a sense of separation from others resulting from less-than-meaningful interactions. For example, have you ever received an e-mail from someone and had no clue as to what they were trying to say, so you turned your attention to other things? Or perhaps you left a message for someone to answer a question, and when they responded their reply was about something completely unrelated. Communications distance turns into a feeling of disconnectedness when there's a lack of shared context and when a less-than-optimal communication mode is used repeatedly. Therefore, the way to close communications distance involves developing common ideas about the places and ways in which we work as well as more selectively using various kinds of communications tools and techniques.

Multitasking

Multitasking increases Virtual Distance because when occupied with many and varied tasks, we tend to feel far away from pretty much everything. We're so focused on our activities that others often get pushed aside in our minds. And there isn't a person we know who isn't overwhelmed with things to do these days. Because we *can* do more, we're doing more. Too much multitasking creates a sense of distance between us. This matters *most* when Virtual Distance is high in other areas.

Readiness Distance

Readiness distance is the feeling of detachment that grows when technical support can't fix problems with machines and other devices in a timely manner. Most likely, you've already experienced readiness distance. It would've happened while you waited for a technical glitch to be fixed during a videoconference, a webinar, a conference call, a presentation, a demonstration of software, or some other technically dependent event. Readiness distance rises when things don't work and there's little to no support or cooperation.

Distribution Asymmetry

Distribution asymmetry is an uneven dispersion of people within any given team or organization. This patchy array of resources causes people to feel as though they're further away than they may really be. In one case, teams consist of a lot of individuals working remotely in their homes or other non-corporate locations. This situation often produces a sense of isolation among individuals. In another case, distribution asymmetry can arise when there are a lot of people located in one centralized place, like a headquarters location. And in a third case, both high dispersion and high centralization can exist within the same team; some members in the hinterlands and some at headquarters. In this case, not only can far-flung resources feel isolated, but those at headquarters usually become somewhat cocooned and have trouble seeing beyond their own views. Distribution asymmetry creates a sense of being far away from others either by virtue of isolation or too many people residing in one place where there's a lot of power.

Summary—Operational Distance

Operational distance causes people to mentally shut others out as they try to make their way through harried and sometimes difficult days. Most of the time, operational distance intensifies without conscious awareness. However, we know that it does a lot of harm. But, out of all the pieces in the Virtual Distance Model, operational distance is the most easily controlled by an alert and skilled leader.

AFFINITY DISTANCE

Affinity distance (see Figure A.4) is what develops when we don't establish the kinds of personal relationships that satisfy our social needs. When this facet of Virtual Distance is high, a powerful psychological wall bars effective collaboration.

There are four relationship dynamics that come together to create an affinity vacuum:

1. Cultural distance
2. Social distance
3. Relationship distance
4. Interdependence distance

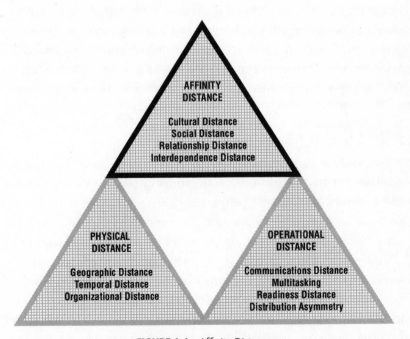

FIGURE A.4   Affinity Distance

Moral values—personal set of absolute values used as a guide to know what is"right"versus "wrong." When these are violated, we tend to take drastic action. Whistleblowers exemplify when moral values have been crossed at work.

Work values—the internal road map we create to guide us through work made up of our personal values as they are applied to our individual work habits and styles.

Personal values—the internal road map we create for ourselves based on internalization of group values combined with our own unique worldviews

Cultural Values—group values that arise from being part of various communities both at home and at work

FIGURE A.5   Values Stack

Cultural Distance

Cultural distance represents differences in team member values (the internal rules or guidelines that direct our lives and decision making), which come in many forms and are described in Figure A.5.

Affinity is difficult if not impossible to establish if some or all of our values are out of sync. Cultural distance is at the top of the list when it comes to escalating affinity distance and stunting healthy relationship growth in the virtual workforce. Fixing cultural distance consists of developing shared value systems and re-imagining values in light of others that may appear to be different but, in many ways, are much the same.

Social Distance

Social distance develops when people hold a range of different social positions. Status within and across groups is relevant to any form of collaboration. For example, people have different levels of status in local communities, and these striations are influenced by factors such as political position and wealth, among others. The truth is that some get more consideration than others, fostering a sense of unfairness that increases social distance. It's easy to see how harmful social distance can be and how difficult it is to manage, as it involves identity and ego, two of the most fragile aspects of human psychology. However, when team members feel they're on a level playing field based on competence and their shared role in the work effort, they're much more likely to meet goals.

Relationship Distance

Relationship distance is the extent to which you and others lack relationship connections from past work initiatives. If you belong to any kind of online social networking system, you can usually see pictures that show the number of direct ties you have with someone and the number of indirect ties with many others. These relationships, known as strong ties and weak ties, respectively, are needed for healthy communication and relationship building. When there are no historical ties between two or more people or only a scattered few, then one feels more distant from the rest. Relationship distance manifests as a sense of unfamiliarity. When people don't have any idea of who others are or lack any indirect connections, it's difficult to establish trust without having to build a relationship from scratch, and as we've learned already, our ability to do so in the Digital Age is challenged quite a bit by forces outside of our control, for example, being near or having time to devote to such efforts.

Interdependence Distance

Interdependence distance describes the psychology behind team member commitment to one another—or a lack thereof. If individuals or groups don't believe they're mutually dependent on each other, then motivation wanes and projects drift. When there is no shared vision or linked missions, a feeling of "not being part of the action," so to speak, sabotages the desire to actively participate. Interdependence distance can hurt companies quite badly because people are too detached from one another—not in terms of physicality but in terms of their connection to a shared vision.

Summary—Affinity Distance

Affinity distance arises from a lack of commonality between our values systems and styles, social behaviors, relationship histories, and worldviews, or mental pictures of the world. The four affinity distance areas represent those dynamics that shape us as human beings.

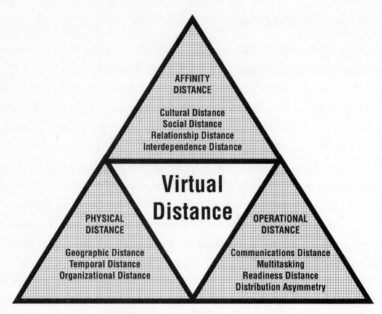

FIGURE A.6   The Virtual Distance Model

They provide the context in which we develop and retain relationships; therefore, within virtual teamwork, it's of primary importance to reduce affinity distance.

THE VIRTUAL DISTANCE MODEL

We hope that this brief overview provides a reasonably good understanding of Virtual Distance (see Figure A.6). Virtual Distance is a model made up of a trio of distance-causing features in the virtual workplace, each of which can be active one at a time, but more often than not, all at the same time. Understanding Virtual Distance is one important step that leaders can take to be more effective in managing organizations in the virtual, digital world.

Index